Presented to the
Ironside Memorial Library
Bryan College
by
Darryl Bradley

THE QUAKER CONTRIBUTION

The Quaker Contribution

HAROLD LOUKES

THE MACMILLAN COMPANY
NEW YORK

Library of Congress Catalog Card Number: 65-18468

PRINTED IN GREAT BRITAIN

CONTENTS

I

The Sects under Judgement

THE PRODIGAL sects are beginning to come home, as they discover that the far country of their freedom is in some curious way short of food: food for their own nourishing, and food to give to the hungry. Both these motives are powerfully at work in the ecumenical movement: the discovery that Christians are making that the other sects, whom they thought they could do without, have sources of life that they begin to hunger for; and the discovery that a sect in isolation cannot meet the questions pressing in upon it from the non-Christian world.

The home-coming is being conducted at different levels: by leaders and 'experts', discussing problems of structure and theology, and by the 'congregation in the street', as it meets neighbouring congregations in common worship, or service, or fellowship. At both these levels progress, slow but unmistakable, is being made. But before either of these approaches can reach an understanding unity, there is need for the sects to give an account of themselves, to answer the question: What, after all, are you up to? Why and how did you come to move outside the established structure at the time when you split away? What were you saying then? And are you still saying the same thing? What have you learnt on the way, as you have tried to live by yourselves? Have you any warnings for other Christians on the problems of your special kind of isolation? And what have you found, by the way, that you are sure must be kept alive when the day finally comes that sees you march back into the Catholic Church, with all flags flying?

Behind these questions there is a wider challenge, flung down by the explosion of the 'religionless Christianity' argument, the challenge to demonstrate, in the language men use when they talk together, what is the meaning of the jargon that Christians in their sects use among themselves. The 'Honest-to-God debate' is at root a scrutiny of language, not merely the words to be used but the images behind the words. Whatever be its ultimate fate, the new theology presents an effort at translation of terms that have demonstrably lost much of their meaning and power, an attempt to 'identify the referent' when we use inherited imagery. If the old notions will not 'go into newspeak' then either we have lost the meaning of the notions, or 'newspeak' is inadequate to serious affairs, and must be extended. But it would be intolerable if we could not talk about serious affairs at all without learning an archaic dialect of 'oldspeak'. If modern man is as hopelessly lost as some Christians say he is, he needs someone to speak to him in his own tongue, not someone who says, First master our Grammar of the Christian Tongue. 'So likewise ye, except ye utter by the tongue words easy to be understood, how shall it be known what is spoken? for ye shall speak into the air.'[1]

This challenge, to bring our sectarian statement to the bar of 'truth', has always been there. Coleridge saw it clearly enough when he wrote, 'He who begins by loving Christianity better than truth will proceed by loving his own sect or church better than Christianity, and end in loving himself better than all.'[2]

[1] I Cor. 14.9.
[2] *Aids to Reflection*, Moral and Religious Aphorisms, XXIV.

The pages that follow offer an account of the experience of the Society of Friends, whose seventeenth-century search for an open and dynamic imagery produced in the eighteenth century a closed and static imagery; and who have had in the last hundred years to conduct a private search for the rediscovery of their early findings. It begins in controversy beside which our present-day exchanges are as the cooing of doves, and it ends in a tolerance that may be suspected of indifference to the real issues. It begins in ruthless iconoclasm, and ends in a slightly puzzled respectability. It begins in reckless openness to all men and to all their affairs, and ends in a self-critical and rapidly disappearing peculiarity.

The *apologia* must come as a story, for apart from one ingenious failure Friends have never sought to set out a reasoned system of belief. Their whole case, indeed, rests on the assertion that belief is too deep a matter to be contained in reasoned systems: that 'belief' is trust, and not merely a set of 'notions', action and not merely assent to the correct. Friends would say with Kierkegaard that 'the highest of all is not to understand the highest but to act upon it'. How far they would accept Kierkegaard's further claim, that he recognizes 'an imperative of understanding' and 'that through it one can work upon man', we shall see as the story proceeds.

It is a story that must, as far as possible, be told through the mouths of the characters, for it is a story of personal experience, some novel and adventurous, some tame and fearful, but always 'personal', and requiring the personal voice for its description. It is therefore a story 'full of quotations', in which the voice can be heard, and lacking for the most part a general theory within which 'the personal' is to be interpreted. For the 'anti-theory' on which the whole adventure is based is the claim that it is *first* in the 'personal' that religious truth is to be found, and only later in the institutions or abstractions from the personal which may become escape-routes from the agonies of choice and encounter.

It is this that Quakerism is 'about'. It is this, said many reformers, that the Reformation was about. The Church, they argued, had become imprisoned in her own institutions, and had become an obstacle to her own purposes. The purposes, it would be agreed by Christians of any colour, are ultimately, in some way, personal. Von Hügel was later to put the matter in terms that many Christians, on both sides of the conflict, would have been able to accept.[1] In our first learning about religion we are dependent on people who interpret it for us, and who 'represent the principle of authority in its simplest form'.

> The little child gets these impressions long before it itself can choose between, or even is distinctly conscious of them; it believes whatever it sees and is told, equally, as so much fact, as something to build on . . . And at this stage the External, Authoritative, Historical, Traditional, Institutional side and function of Religion are everywhere evident . . . Religion is here, above all, a Fact and Thing.

But then comes the time when the tradition needs adjustment in the light of personal experience. It does not entirely fit the individual case. What other men say does not sufficiently explain what *I* have found for myself.

> Here it is the reasoning, argumentative, abstractive side of human nature that begins to come into play . . . this and this is now connected with that and that; this is true or this need not be false, because of that and that. Religion here becomes Thought, System, a Philosophy.

But there is a third stage, in which personal action becomes the centre of life, and external impression and abstract thought drift out to the circumference:

[1] *The Mystical Element of Religion*, London, 1923, vol. i, p. 51.

> For man is necessarily a creature of action, even more than of sensation and of reflection; and in this action . . . he grows and gradually comes to his real self, and gains certain experiences as to the existence and nature and growth of this his own deeper personality.
>
> Man's emotional and volitional, his ethical and spiritual powers, are now in ever fuller motion, and they are met and fed by the third side of religion, the Experimental and Mystical. Here religion is rather felt than seen or reasoned about, is loved and lived rather than analysed, is action and power, rather than either external fact or intellectual verification.

Von Hügel is here offering an account of the religious 'learning process' that takes account of the reformers' case. Among the reformers would be found two different answers. Some would have said, Yes, this is true: but only if the institutions themselves are kept 'pure'. If the first stage is set about with falsehood, the other stages can never be reached. Therefore, reform the Church. But some others would have said, No. The process here is the wrong way round. Religion begins in the 'emotional and volitional', and only when it is realized in that way can it safely proceed to the rational and the institutional.

It was sufficient for the first group to clear from the Church all errors of practice and doctrine, so that within the new, purified institution true learning could take place. The story of the Reformation could be told in these terms: first, the removal of the Pope with his dangerous, final authority, the Mass with its miraculous happening that was supposed to occur even without the personal struggle of the communicant, the images with their false power, the indulgences that could be bought without personal suffering; then the shift from Rome to the English Establishment. But then the process is pressed further, as the Presbyterians reduce priestly authority and seek to shift responsibility to the elders of the congregation. Then goes the central structure of control itself, as the Independents push responsibility out to the local congregations. And at last the Baptists, subtracting infant baptism, pushed responsibility on to the individual, adult member of the congregation, insisting that even his membership was not provided for him, but had to be found, in personal conversion.

The theme in all of this was the purification of institutions: not the abolition of institutions. There were some, even so, who were disappointed, as was Milton with his famous 'New Presbyter is old priest writ large', men who found that even 'purified' institutions had a way of creating institutionalism, of being in their own nature self-defeating. And so there arose the more radical argument, that institutions should be abolished altogether, that men must start with the Experimental and Volitional, must look inwards in total commitment to private experience.

A story typical of many was that of John Gratton (1645-1712),[1] who tried all the sects, only to be driven to reject one after another as they searched for an institution 'pure' enough for their own quest.

> The Episcopalian Priests came in their white surplices and read common-prayers . . . I saw they had the form without the power . . . their worship to be in ceremony and outward things without life.
>
> The Presbyterian priests, whom I had so much esteemed and admired, made their farewell sermons and left us . . . They ought not to be silent at man's command if the Lord had sent and commanded them to preach. So I left them.
>
> When the people sang Psalms in the steeple-house I durst not sing the same lines or sayings of David, it would have been a lie in my mouth.

[1] One of the earliest Quaker preachers, in Derbyshire and the Midlands. 'I ran to and fro,' he writes, 'and Truth prospered gloriously.'

> I went to Chesterfield to seek out and meet those people called Independents for I liked the name, seeing nothing at all in man as man to depend on, but they depended only upon the death and sufferings of Christ in his own body and did not come to see him nor his appearance in themselves to be their life, for I read the Scripture and say 'if any man hath not the Spirit of Christ, he is none of his'.
>
> I found a people called Anabaptists . . . I thought they came nearest the Scriptures of any I had yet tried . . . After they came out of the water . . . I saw no appearance of the spirit of newness of life or power . . . their baptism being only with water which can only wash away the filth of flesh.[1]

So far this is a story of a choice among institutions, the search for a system that did not pollute the fountains of truth. But in the end Gratton rejected them all just because they *were* institutions, and carried their inevitable external marks: they presented him with other men's statements before he had found his own; and he found peace at last only with the Society of Friends, who left him in silence to meet experience for himself:

> There was little said in that meeting but I sat still in it, and was bowed in spirit before the Lord, and felt him with me and with Friends, and saw that they had their minds retired, and waited to feel his presence and power to operate in their hearts and that they were spiritual worshippers who worship God in spirit and in truth and I was sensible that they felt and tasted of the Lord's goodness as at that time I did, and though few words were spoken, yet I was well satisfied with the meeting. And there arose a sweet melody that went through the meeting and the presence of the Lord was in the midst of us and more true comfort, refreshment and satisfaction did I meet with from the Lord in that meeting than ever I had in any meeting in all my life before.[2]

[1] John Gratton, *Journal* (1720), pp. 34-87.

[2] Ib., 41-2.

The question John Gratton was concerned to answer was the question: Where do you *start*? Do you start in the institutions—the white surplices, the psalms of David, propositions about the death of Christ—and, as it were, make them the goals of your learning? If so, you are entangled in what will be meaningless to you, 'forms without power'. No, he says, you must start where you are, having your mind 'retired', waiting to 'feel his presence and power' in your heart. You explore the present and the inward, or you will be held prisoner by the past and the outward.

There is more to this than a mere preference for one kind of institution over another. There is a radical argument about the nature of knowledge and the learning process. We are familiar today with the educational conflict between 'words' and 'things', between 'learning the grammar' and 'starting with the facts'. The John Grattons of the seventeenth century were for things rather than words, for facts rather than grammar. In this, they were guided by the analogy with science. 'He that desireth to acquire any art or science,' says Barclay,[1] 'seeketh first those means by which that art or science is obtained. If we ought to do so in things natural and earthly, how much more then in things spiritual?'

Beginning with authoritative statements from other men, he continues, is dangerous, and may produce life-long illusion:

> Thus when a man first proposeth to himself the knowledge of God . . . he . . . (not having then a distinct discerning) through forwardness embraceth any thing that brings present ease. If . . . through the reverence he bears to certain per-

[1] Robert Barclay (1648-1690), of Scottish Presbyterian and Catholic background, to which no doubt he owed the motive for his *Apology for the true Christian Divinity* (1676), the only serious attempt at a Quaker theology.

> sons . . . he fall upon any principle or means, by which he apprehends he may come to know God, and so doth center himself, it will be hard to remove him thence again, how wrong soever they may be: for the first anguish being over, he becomes more hardy; and the enemy being near, creates a false peace, and a certain confidence, which is strengthened by the mind's unwillingness to enter again into new doubtfulness, or the former anxiety of a search.[1]

The significant phrase here is 'unwillingness to enter again into new doubtfulness': the reluctance to start again, experimentally, without certainties or comfort from the tradition.

The Quaker theme is this extreme statement of the Reformation: that true religion consists not in certainty but in search, not old conviction but 'new doubtfulness'. In the end there was a 'new certainty' to be discovered, but it was a certainty of a different kind from the old: no longer fixed and hardened into institutions and creeds, but infinitely more powerful because it reached the centre of human being.

The Quaker story is thus the story of a group of people who trusted to the inward and rejected the outward. And the question we now ask this people is, What happened when you put your trust in this alone? How did you get on without the traditional elements that other Christians have claimed they needed for their learning? And do you still feel that this is all there is to be said?

[1] *Apology*, Proposition 1.

II

The Son of 'Righteous Christer'

THE QUAKER story begins with the story of George Fox (1624-1691). Friends have sometimes looked back on him, in their nostalgic moods, as founder and father-figure. 'What would George Fox have said about *this?*' they still sometimes say to each other when the talk becomes a little small. But he is not primarily a father-figure: he is rather the first experimenter, the man who entered a field of experience that other Friends were to enter, who made first the discoveries they were later to make for themselves. His gifts were the empiricist's gifts: a persistent and rather disconcerting honesty, so that he saw the Emperor without his clothes and said so; the deep personal stability within whirling feeling; the sense that the human quest was of supreme importance.

His honesty he derived from a simple Puritan home: from his father ('Righteous Christer', his neighbours called him), 'a weaver, an honest man, and . . . the seed of God in him'[1] and from his mother, 'an upright woman . . . of the stock of the martyrs'. His obstinate questing began early[2] when he saw that the simple integrity of his parents was not shared by all men:

> In my very young years I had a gravity and stayedness of mind and spirit not usual in children, insomuch that, when I

[1] *The Journal of George Fox*, ed. T. C. Nickalls, 1952, p. 1.
[2] In 1643, at the age of nineteen.

> have seen old men carry themselves lightly and wantonly towards each other, I have had a dislike thereof risen in my heart, and have said within myself, 'If ever I come to be a man, surely I should not do so nor be so wanton.'

From this point of departure, he was to become increasingly sensitive to the difference between 'profession' and action, ostensible faith and manifest works; and to be increasingly reluctant to accept counsel or expect guidance from men more divided in spirit than he was himself. He was noted, even in his teens, for the simplicity and integrity of his own speech:

> I used in my dealings the word 'Verily', and it was a common saying among people that knew me, 'If George says "Verily" there is no altering him.'[1]

Fox, and Friends after him, were to regard this integrity as the first condition of the religious life.

> The Lord taught me to be faithful in all things and to act faithfully in two ways, viz. inwardly to God and outwardly to man, and to keep to 'yea' and 'nay' in all things . . . and that my words should be few and savoury, seasoned with grace.[2]

Language, he was maintaining, as he linked his 'faithfulness to God' with 'faithfulness to man', must be faithful to experience and correspond closely with the facts.

But this honesty of language, he argued, must be matched by honesty of looking. If words are to be used faithfully, things must be seen clearly, so the eye must be single, the life of the observer must be uncluttered, open to clear impressions. Thus he demanded of himself, as the second condition of exploration, a measure of austerity, the rejection of luxury and unnecessary pleasures:

> I might not eat and drink to make myself wanton but for health, using the creatures in their service, as servants in their places, to the glory of him that hath created them.[3]

[1] Ib., p. 1. [2] Ib., p. 2. [3] Ib., p. 2.

These old men, carrying themselves 'lightly and wantonly', were not taking life seriously: the quest for the roots of existence was a more serious business than they realized.

Honesty of tongue, and simplicity of seeing: these are the prime conditions of human communication. But at first they were to drive Fox into a spiritual desert in which he was lost to human comfort. The episodes that cut him off from other men were trivial, almost ridiculous in themselves, important only to Fox. One was a chance encounter with a cousin and his friend, who 'professed' Puritanism, but challenged George to a drinking bout.

> agreeing together that he that would not drink should pay all. They grieved me very much, having never had such a thing put to me before by any sort of people; wherefore I rose up to be gone, and putting my hand into my pocket I took out a groat and laid it down upon the table before them and said, 'If it be so, I'll leave you.' So I went away; and when I had done what business I had to do, I returned home, but did not go to bed that night, nor could not sleep, but sometimes walked up and down, and sometimes prayed and cried to the Lord, who said unto me, 'Thou seest how young people go together into vanity and old people into the earth; and thou must forsake all, both young and old, and keep out of all, and be as a stranger unto all.'[1]

He sought counsel from priests and 'professors', but they were not honest:

> I was sensible they did not possess what they professed.

He listened to the learned, but decided that learning was irrelevant to the true issue:

> The Lord opened unto me that being bred at Oxford or Cambridge was not enough to fit and qualify men to be ministers of Christ.[2]

He went to church, but it was 'opened' to him that God

[1] Ib., p. 3. [2] Ib., p. 7.

'who made the world did not dwell in temples made with hands'.[1]

And so, shrinking from professions that did not match possessions, he arrived at loneliness and despair:

> And I fasted much, and walked abroad in solitary places many days, and often took my Bible and went and sat in hollow trees and lonesome places till night came on; and frequently in the night walked mournfully about by myself, for I was a man of sorrows in the times of the first workings of the Lord in me.[2]

And there he remained until his last hopes of counsel from any human agency had gone:

> And when all my hopes in them and in all men were gone, so that I had nothing outwardly to help me, nor could tell what to do, then, Oh then, I heard a voice which said, 'There is one, even Christ Jesus, that can speak to thy condition.' And when I heard it my heart did leap for joy. Then the Lord did let me see why there was none upon the earth that could speak to my condition, namely, that I might give him all the glory; for all are concluded under sin, and shut up in unbelief as I had been, that Jesus Christ might have the pre-eminence, who enlightens and gives grace, and faith, and power. Thus, when God doth work, who shall let it? And this I knew experimentally.[3]

'Experimentally'. Fox was asserting that his 'method' had worked: the refusal to accept authorities that failed to convince, the loneliness, the obstinate standing by his own insight, the patient persistence until he reached a place of certainty. There were still to be doubts and inner struggle, still, as Barclay would say, the 'anxiety of a search'; but from this time on there was to be no doubt about the need for search, and the reward of doubt and struggle.

And as he had found, so should other men find, not resting in the institutional, but penetrating the personal:

[1] Ib., p. 8. [2] Ib., p. 9. [3] Ib., p. 11.

> And I saw professors, priests and people were whole and at ease in that condition which was my misery, and they loved that which I would have been rid of. But the Lord did stay my desires upon himself from whom my help came, and my care was cast upon him alone. Therefore, all wait patiently upon the Lord, whatsoever condition you be in; wait in the grace and truth that comes by Jesus; for if ye so do, there is a promise to you, and the Lord God will fulfil it in you.[1]

And so Fox saw his task as the calling of his generation to 'experimentalism', both the experimentalism of first-hand experience and the experimentalism of demonstrable consequence, of a deeply effective personal experience that would work a recognizable change in the personal life. And so he plunged into the conversion of Christians to the new 'method'.

In this he saw his role, not as the founder of a sect, but as the evangelist to all the sects of the gospel of empiricism.

> And I was to bring people off from all the world's religions, which are vain, that they might know the pure religion, and might visit the fatherless, the widows and the strangers, and keep themselves from the spots of the world . . . And I was to bring people off from Jewish ceremonies, and from heathenish fables, and from men's inventions and windy doctrines, by which they blowed the people about this way and the other way, from sect to sect; and all their beggarly rudiments, with their schools and colleges for making ministers of Christ, who are indeed ministers of their own making but not of Christ's; and from all their images and crosses, and sprinkling of infants, with all their holy days . . . and all their vain traditions, which they had gotten up since the apostles' days, which the Lord's power was against, and in the dread and authority thereof I was moved to declare against them all, and against all that preached and not freely, as being such as had not received freely from Christ.[2]

[1] Ib., p. 12.

[2] Ib., p. 35.

This ambitious vocation was confirmed by the discovery of groups of discontented Christians who had withdrawn from normal church life and gathered together in a kind of undirected expectancy, and vaguely accepting the name Seekers, and meeting for the unplanned exchange of 'anything that arose in any one of their minds' that they thought 'savoured of a Divine spring'[1] but for much of the time waiting in silence. The discovery of these Christians uneasy as he had been, trusting in the method by which he had found his own vision, must have seemed to Fox justification of a powerful kind; and their response to his preaching was so immediate that almost without intention he found himself leading a sect: not, they thought, a sect for all time, but a sect for all men, a sect against sectarianism, a group bound together only in a common discovery and a common zeal to open the way for the Church to find her own hidden life.

In the end the vision failed, and the Quaker movement turned into a sect after all. The reasons were various. Partly, the fault lay with the limitations of Fox's own personality. He never understood how much he had learnt 'on authority', nor how a pure vision may be transmitted by those who, in the practice of their daily life, fall short of its perfection. The innovator is inevitably impatient with the tradition; and however persuasive his preaching, he is likely to alienate, rather than convince, the traditionalists. It was perhaps inevitable that a movement led by Fox would appeal to those lost as he had been lost, but at some point arouse the opposition of those who did not feel lost, but felt menaced by an attack on their familiar ways of thought. Fox's outspokenness, his honesty, was not tactful; his interruptions of church services were provocative; and

[1] William Penn, in his Preface to Fox's *Journal*.

it was not long before clergy dreaded his arrival. He was soon in prison, for interrupting a priest (who stood, Fox tells us, in his pulpit 'like a great lump of earth') to deny his claim that the 'Scriptures were the touchstone and judge' of doctrine in religion. '"Oh, no, it is not the Scriptures" . . . but . . . the Holy Spirit.' And so he was put into prison. And so he was again, eight times, for a total of six years. And other Friends suffered in the same way. In the nineteen years from the accession of Charles II to the passing of the Toleration Act (1689) twelve thousand of them went to prison, and over three hundred died there. They were committed because they preached their heresy in churches or in the open air, because they refused to abandon public worship, because they refused to take oaths, or remove their hats in the presence of the magistrates, or because they were suspected of treason: for, in the end, obstinacy in the refusal to accept the outward forms of religion and good manners which they regarded as obstacles to the inward vision.

It was not long before the task of evangelism, the support of the persecuted, and the nurture of growing congregations demanded a measure of organization which had certainly not been foreseen, and which was to constitute the decisive shift from 'movement' to 'sect'. Here, plainly, was the capital problem of Quakerism: the devising of a structure to defend the personal search, to organize but not to mechanize, to guide but not to direct. At the outset there was little more 'organization' than that provided by a handful of travelling Friends. As Fox had evoked community by travelling about preaching, so other Friends moved about the country extending and establishing it. 'The travelling ministering Friends', writes Hugh Doncaster,[1]

[1] In *Quaker Organization and Business Meetings*, London, 1958, p. 10.

'were like the blood circulating in the young body of the Society, and enabled a surprising uniformity of faith and practice to be developed very quickly.' This was 'unity by personal encounter', community by communication. As the local groups began to find themselves, however, they needed something more permanent, and in 1653 William Dewsbury advised meetings to choose one or two 'most grown in the Power and Life, in the pure discerning in the Truth',[1] to exercise a special responsibility for the maintaining of the group life, to arrange meetings for worship, and to watch over the conduct of Friends. Two years later Fox was to write to such Friends, saying 'All ye, whom the Lord hath made overseers over his church in your several places, be faithful to the Lord and watch over the flock of Christ with all diligence.'[2]

At first glance, the recognition of 'elders' seems to be a denial of Quaker principle: is this not, one might ask, capitulation to the worldly principle of authority and status? The time was to come when the status of elders and overseers would be open to some such criticism; but at the outset, there was no conflict with principle. They did, indeed, constitute a special illustration of principle: the principle that religious experience begins in the personal and not in the institutional. Early Friends were uninhibitedly hostile to 'hireling priests' educated at Oxford and Cambridge but with no message for their flock, who had learnt what to say but did not know what they were talking about. This was to create an institution without the 'person', to grant status that did not correspond with reality. Then start from the other end, said Friends. Begin with the personal, with the member of the meeting who has demonstrated that he does know what he is talking

[1] Dewsbury, *Works*, 1689, p. 1.
[2] Fox, *Epistles*, 1698, No. 83 (p. 75).

about, and has a word of guidance and wisdom: and 'institutionalize' him, but only to the degree that will make it possible for him to say it.

These elders or overseers, it must be remembered, gave their counsel within the face-to-face group in which the members knew each other and lived, in a measure, a common life. And this creation of a system of face-to-face meetings that constituted the 'authority-in-defence-of-freedom' not only enabled the Society of Friends to survive (which, after all, might have been very unprincipled of them) but offered a positive and creative definition of freedom. Friends were not interested in 'freedom' if all that was meant by that term was 'permission not to'. They were only interested in freedom of worship, to discover each other at the personal level and to dis-cover the depths of their own personality. They were not saying that human life was adequately lived if it merely avoided the impersonal: only if it released the personal. And though elders were, in fact, to exercise certain negative powers of discipline, their prime task was communication, initiative, and insight. They were not so much 'appointed to status' as —and it is still a favourite Quaker term for appointments— 'released'.

Soon after this modest beginning of organization, it became necessary to face another problem. The primary group, sufficiently strengthened by its elders to enable the members to 'know one another . . . in the things that endure', can count on a certain unity of purpose in which the group life does not move far away from the individual life. The members, however radically they reject creeds and statements and external commands, however deep they go into their private experience, will, in practice, keep each other together. But how are the separate groups to be prevented from drifting apart? If there are to be no rules of church practice, how are the various meetings to remain a church?

There soon grew up—at first at random, later to be planned and ordered—a series of 'General Meetings', held at intervals of a few weeks, a month, or several times a year.

> The purpose of these meetings was both spiritual and practical. The gathering together of Friends from other meetings for worship and fellowship and mutual encouragement was particularly important when they faced bitter opposition from their neighbours. But they were also to care for their poor, to help the aged and infirm, to provide employment for those who had lost their jobs because of their faith, or given them up 'by reason of the evil therein' which now was seen. The aim was 'that there may not be a beggar amongst us, nor any whose souls need be oppressed with care for food or raiment' . . . Such meetings soon had the responsibility of keeping registers of births, marriages and deaths . . . and . . . the responsibility for guiding the flock and admonishing those who 'walked disorderly', but much tenderness and patience was to be exercised before public condemnation or disownment were advised.[1]

It was to be George Fox's own contribution to the permanence of the Society to turn these irregular meetings into a systematic structure that would minimize the danger of over-authoritarian leadership, and make the 'authority' of the Society at once strong enough to counter whimsy and yet sensitive to individual need and insight. Thus, says Fox,

> the Lord opened to me and let me see what I must do and how I must order and establish the men and women's monthly and quarterly meetings in all the nation, and other nations to do the same, or write to them where I came not.[2]

Though the detail has changed in a few trifles, the dynamic structure has remained to this day; and though anything

[1] Hugh Doncaster, op. cit., p. 12. [2] Journal, p. 111.

operated by human beings is open to be frustrated by stupidity, laziness, pride and ill-temper, the essential purpose of the fluid structure has been achieved. Instead of breaking up into isolated groups, Friends have remained curiously homogeneous, in consequence of the ceaseless to-and-fro of members, important and unimportant, vocal and silent, between the meetings. Monthly Meetings, grouping several particular meetings, have in general done the work of the Society in a small district: the care of the meeting houses, and of the members themselves. Quarterly Meetings, covering one or two counties, have existed largely for the sake of the 'group mind', for the sharing of 'concerns' and the consideration of the larger issues facing Friends in the world.

The structure was virtually complete by 1678, from which year a Yearly Meeting, concerned with 'the public affairs of Friends throughout the nation' has been held regularly. By this year there was also in existence a national committee, Meeting for Sufferings, at first concerned with the problems arising out of the persecution, but gradually to become an executive committee of the Society, meeting to this day under its original name, but now with an agenda ranging over the whole field of Quaker activity.

It is a structure that is open to the humblest member of the smallest meeting, but at the same time carries an authority that bears upon the most self-confident of its members. Nobody can be sure what the group, small or large, will say: everybody is aware that it will say something. It is, as many active Friends would testify, at once a sobering and a challenging thought, that the Society is open, waiting, for the individual leading; but equally open, waiting, to take hold of the leading and transmute it, if need be, and certainly to take it in to the purpose of the community.

III

Meeting the Light

AS I have begun to tell the Quaker story, it has appeared as a series of rejections and negations: the rejection of priests and presbyters, of temples and 'steeple-houses', of creeds and formal statements, of the safeguards of hierarchic discipline. But Friends did not think of themselves as pulling down, so much as moving on. They were engaged in breaking, it is true, but not in 'breaking up' so much as 'breaking out'.

The 'professors', argued Fox, had stopped short of the goal. The language they used, the level on which they thought and spoke and lived, was below the true level. It was they, he would have said, who lived in negatives: in 'darkness', in 'the contrary', in 'the Deceit'.

> Keep in the Power of the Lord which will keep all the contrary down and out.
>
> The Lord God of Power give thee Wisdom, Courage, Manhood and Boldness to thresh down all Deceit.[1]

The negative was the formal, in word or rite, which concealed the necessity of naked living:

> I find my heart is full of deceit, and I exceedingly fear to be beguiled (as I have been) and to be seduced into a form without power, into a profession before I possess the Truth.[2]

[1] Fox, *Epistles*, 180 (1659); 113 (1656).
[2] Anthony Pearson, *Letters etc. of Early Friends*, p. 2.

Margaret Fell, who was later to marry George Fox, would have said the same:

> I was one that sought after the best things, being desirous to serve God . . . and was enquiring after the way of the Lord, and went often to hear the best ministers that came into our parts . . . This I hope I did well in, but often I feared was short of the right way . . .

But then she heard Fox speak on the 'circumcision of the heart' and 'Christ the Light of the World':

> And then he went on, and opened the Scriptures, and said, 'The Scriptures were the prophets' words and Christ's and the apostles' words, and what as they spoke they enjoyed and possessed and had it from the Lord.' And said, 'Then what had any to do with the Scriptures, but as they came to the spirit that gave them forth? You will say, Christ saith this, and the apostles say this; but what canst thou say? Art thou a Child of Light and hast walked in the Light, and what thou speakest is it inwardly from God?' And I cried in my spirit to the Lord, 'We are all thieves, we are all thieves, we have taken the Scriptures in words and know nothing of them in ourselves.'[1]

Religious machinery, whether the machinery of church government or the imagery of theological or scriptural statement was 'deceit' if men rested in it, failing to 'come to the spirit that gave them forth'. This 'deceit' was not so much to be reformed, or argued with, as left behind. The rejection was to be the sign and means of progress, as a Latin scholar one day comes to 'reject' his primer on his way to the living Latin. Quaker propaganda was full of biblical quotation, but not by way of an appeal to authority so much as a persuasive device. Those who listened to them took the Bible as authority: Friends appealed to it to destroy its authority. It was not statements that carried the Christian meaning, said Friends, but life.

[1] Margaret Fox, quoted in George Fox, *Journal*, 1694, p. ii.

> It is not opinion, or speculation, or notions of what is true, or assent to or the subscription of articles or propositions, though never so soundly worded that . . . makes a man a true believer or a true Christian. But it is a conformity of mind and practice to the will of God, in all holiness of conversation, according to the dictates of this Divine principle of Light and Life in the soul which denotes a person truly a child of God.[1]

In all this Friends were turning their backs on the second of von Hügel's states, as in their church order they were turning their backs on the first. Religion as an inherited system of thought was just as dangerous, they argued, as an inherited system of church order and ritual practice: intellectual machinery as much a 'Saul's armour' as institutional machinery. And just as they were not interested in merely improving the institutional machinery, but only in escaping from it, so they were not interested in reforming theology, but only in starting again from a new point of departure. It is significant that Friends showed no interest in the Cambridge Platonists, who were engaged in bringing theology up to date, making new systems more congenial to the contemporary mind. George Fox met Henry More, on one occasion, but afterwards More observed, 'I never met a man so like brass'.

What Friends did was to replace 'notions', conceptual thought about religion, with emotive metaphor, imagery that would stir the feelings and will but would defy analysis at the rational level. The metaphors bubble out in Fox's writings, continually touching off 'lines of feeling', never setting off lines of thought. Truth, he said, was the Witness of God, the Royal Seed, the Power and Seed of God, the Life and Seed of God, the Wisdom, swept, cool and pure, the Springs of Life, the Truth's Voice, the Heavenly Dignity,

[1] William Penn, *A Key opening the way to every common understanding, sect.* 11.

Truth in the Inward Parts, that Love which bears all things. Two images which recur, and between them bear most of the weight of evocation, are 'Seed' and 'Light'. Later 'Light' was to become a cliché, and lose much of its force, but for early Friends it was powerfully emotive, with its image of an active principle working against darkness; and 'Seed', with its image of new life bursting out from the hidden depths, was frequently used. Barclay throws the images together in a heap that forbids analysis:

> By this seed, grace and word of God and light wherewith we say everyone is enlightened . . . we understand a spiritual, heavenly, invisible principle in which God as Father, Son and Spirit dwells, a measure of which divine and glorious life is in all men as a seed which of its own nature draws, invites and inclines to God.[1]

In all this vivid but imprecise metaphor, there is no hint of the naturalism or humanism or rationalism into which the bald phrase 'Inner Light', when robbed of its emotive power, so easily sinks. The metaphysic behind the language is a poet's metaphysic, vague and unmanageable; but there *is* a metaphysic: an adumbration of unredeemed, meaningless life into which the seed brings a new principle, drawing sustenance from the merely human, but in its own mysterious pattern a novelty from beyond, a pattern the merely human cannot invent; and of a cosmic struggle between substance and shadow, multiplicity and unity, change and eternity. The Light, says Fox,

> is the Word of Life, the Word of Peace, the Word of Reconciliation, which makes of twain one new man and if ye do abide there, there is no division but unity in the life . . . Therefore in the Light wait where the unity is, where the peace is, where the Oneness with the Father and Son is, where there is no Rent nor Division.[2]

[1] *Apology*, p. 137.

[2] *Epistle* 115 (1656).

This is no new individualism, in which men 'follow their own lights'. It is an assertion that the 'one' may be encountered, directly, at first hand, by all.

> See if you do find something in your understandings made manifest, which is Eternal, to guide your minds out of all external things which wither away and fade.[1]

It is an experience of concreteness, bringing men back from abstractions:

> In that dwell which doth bring out of the Shadows, types, traditions.[2]

The Light *was*, says Fox, in the idiom of the Fourth Gospel:

> For this Light was before Time and is in Time.
> In that live which was before enmity was.[3]

The nature of the 'Light' itself is never discussed. It was, Friends might have said, 'beyond', and out of reach of our minds; and to argue about it was not only futile but dangerous, for the argument would divert our attention from the much more urgent demands of 'the beyond in the midst'. Yet the Light was to be known in the personal, in the Person of Christ.

> Everything in the Kingdom, every spiritual thing, refers to Christ and centres in him. His nature, his virtue, his presence, his power makes up all. Indeed he is all in all to a believer, only variously manifested and opened in the heart by the Spirit. He is the volume of the whole book, every leaf and line whereof speaks of him and writes out him in some or other of his sweet and beautiful lineaments. So that if I should yet speak further of other things . . . I should but speak further of his nature brought up, manifested and displaying itself in and through the creatures, by his turning the wheel of his life in their hearts. But my spirit hasteneth

[1] *Epistle* 19 (1652). [2] Ib. 72 (1654). [3] Ib. 111 (1656); 147 (1657).

> from words . . . (that it) may sink in spirit into the feeling of the life itself, and may learn what it is to enjoy it there and to be comprehended of it, and cease striving to know or comprehend concerning it.[1]

Friends have sometimes set out to define their Christology, and to grapple with the problem of the relationships between the 'inward' and the 'historic' Christ. They have never succeeded. Early Friends would have said not only that they would not succeed, but that they ought not to try. Here was an 'object' to be recognized, not a concept to be theorized. Their method was Hamlet's method: 'Look on this picture and on that.' There was no more to be said, except to describe to each other what happened as he 'turned the wheel of his life in their hearts'. Friends assumed, rather than argued, the uniqueness of Christ, which they expressed as a difference of 'measure'. In man, the Light was never completely known: in Jesus it was 'without measure'. Fox quotes Saint John: 'God giveth not the Spirit by measure unto him', and charges men to be aware that their own capacity for response is not unlimited:

> Let no Friends go beyond their own measure given them of God, nor rejoice in another man's line made ready to their hands.
>
> Mind the pure Life of God in you according to your measures to guide you up to God.[2]

But in their measure—and this was to be another grand theme of Quakerism—all men were capable of receiving the Light, not only all men brought up in a Christian environment, but 'all men everywhere'. Only begin where you are, but *begin*, said Friends. Look to the Light, take it seriously, and you will be guided 'up to God'. From this assertion

[1] Isaac Penington, *Works*, 1681, pt. i, pp. 420-1.
[2] *Epistles*, 118 (1656); 69 (1654).

comes a favourite Quaker phrase: 'answering that of God' in other men: the definition of evangelism in terms of dialogue rather than homiletic, of religious discourse as the exchange of experience rather than 'propagation of the Gospel'.

> Answer the witness of God in every man, whether they are the heathen that do not profess Christ, or whether they are such as do profess Christ that have the form of godliness and be out of the Power.[1]
>
> This is the word of the Lord God to you all and a charge to you all in the presence of the living God, be patterns, be examples in all countries, places, islands, nations, wherever you come; that your carriage and life may preach among all sorts of people, and to them; then you will come to walk cheerfully over the world, answering that of God in every one.[2]

[1] *Epistle* 292 (1672).
[2] Fox, letter from prison to 'Friends in the ministry'.

IV

Meeting in the Light

FRIENDS DID not devise their formless form of worship: it 'happened to them' when they were not going to church. Before George Fox brought them his vision and purpose, the groups of Seekers knew they could no longer join church-worship, but did not yet know what they should be doing.

> Now, though many were convinced and did believe the Truth, and divers did no longer join with the priests of the world in their public worship, yet we had no settled or appointed meetings: but on the first days of the week it was the manner of some of us to go to some town where were friendly people and there sit together, and sometimes confer one with another of the dealings of the Lord with us.[1]

It is easy to understand that such 'meetings for comfort' would be strengthening and reassuring to men and women who had followed the path John Gratton was to tread, fleeing from sect to sect, and from 'forms without power'. For the first time they could simply *be*: sit quietly and do nothing, subject to no pressures save their own thoughts and the thoughts of others who had taken flight. They had here a means of support denied to Fox during his solitary struggle, the assurance that they were not abandoned, and that though they were lost, there were others lost with them. We can picture them on Sunday morning, when the

[1] *The First Publishers of Truth*, edited for the Friends' Historical Society by Norman Penney, London, 1907, p. 293.

church bells rang, and all their neighbours set out for church, fidgeting about uneasily at home, perhaps guiltily and anxiously, perhaps opening their Bibles but shutting them again as they found more words that did not 'speak to their condition'; and finally getting up and seizing a hat and walking out to a house where they knew there would be another in like plight; and going quietly in and just thinking, like a family silent with grief, until a thought comes up to the surface and asks to be shared.

It was not long before they moved on from the comfort of relaxation in company to the discovery that the silent form had its special challenge: that it demanded an inner discipline as real as any outer discipline from the liturgy; and they began to charge each other with the need to take the silence seriously:

> The first that enters into the place of your meeting, be not careless, nor wander up and down, either in body or mind, but innocently sit down in some place and turn in thy mind to the light, and wait upon God singly, as if none were present but the Lord . . . Then the next that comes in, let them in simplicity of heart sit down and turn in to the same light, and wait in the Spirit, and so all the rest coming in, in the fear of the Lord, sit down in pure stillness and silence of all flesh, and wait in the light . . . These who are brought to a pure still waiting upon God in the spirit, are come nearer to the Lord than words are; for God is a spirit and in the spirit is he worshipped.[1]

The silence itself was the meeting place. Words might come if they would, but they were not important: they were merely a means to a more living, demanding silence. Richard Davies (1635-1708) describes a meeting in which there was no word spoken, but where the power was strong:

> Though it was silent from words, yet the word of the Lord God was among us; it was as a hammer and a fire; it was

[1] Alexander Parker, *Letters of Early Friends*, p. 365.

> sharper than any two-edged sword; it pierced through our inward parts; it melted and brought us into tears that there was scarcely a dry eye among us. The Lord's blessed power overshadowed our meeting, and I could have said that God alone was Master of that assembly.[1]

'Sharper than any two-edged sword.' This is the central discovery of Quakerism, more fundamental than their lay-structure, or assertions about human nature: this painful difference between the silence of a mere absence of words and the silence of a personal search, conducted in fellowship, at a level deeper than words. It is perhaps the only important element in Quaker life that is entitled to be called a 'discovery' at all, for most of the propositions and practices of early Friends were Puritan commonplaces. But this was new. No Christian group before them had ever cut itself off completely from any trace of liturgical form and trusted only to this.

It has been objected that Friends made a 'form' of their silence: that they were making a sacrament out of physical events—sitting together, the convention that they did not speak until the emotional tension had risen, the nervous tension itself—as surely as other Christians used the symbols of bread and wine. If by 'form' is meant nothing more than the use of the mechanisms of the body-mind, then this 'objection' would be no objection, for the experience of the 'beyond in the midst' must obviously be an experience that at some point has a material effect. It must take hold of the body-mind, and there will be certain physical and mental conditions in which it does so. This, Friends would have said, is precisely our point. We remove the traditional forms because they are inappropriate: they get in the way of the true experience; they are not part of the conditions that must be met. What we object to is not the

[1] Richard Davies, *Journal*, 1752 edn., p. 35.

use of the physical, but the arrangement of physical events that give the impression that they 'work' by themselves, but do not reach the seat of personal experience.

In theory, their objection was unnecessary. The current view on the sacraments, stated in responsible quarters, was careful to guard against materialism or superstition. The transubstantiation battle was over, and the Puritan teaching was directed towards the inward experience rather than the mere performance of the rite:

> Worthy Receivers outwardly partaking of the visible Elements of this Sacrament do then also inwardly by Faith, really and indeed, yet not carnally and corporally, but spiritually, receive and feed upon Christ crucified, and all benefits of his death.[1]

But, Friends insisted, we found the 'elements' distracted us; and only when we left them behind did we begin to 'feed, really and indeed'. They defended their action on the grounds that Jesus had no intention of establishing a new rite. The whole burden of his life and work constituted a warning against rites; and this rite, of which the Church had made something so different from the supper with which he asked to be remembered, was no different from the 'Jewish ceremonies' that the new life brought to an end. The New Covenant which Christ initiated implied an end to all such pre-Christian ceremonial, and the Church had strayed beyond the New Testament experience.

Other Christians were therefore wrong in maintaining their ritual. Isaac Penington, a tender-hearted Friend, thought they might be forgiven: 'I am persuaded the Lord is tender to Persons that do things in tenderness of Heart to him, notwithstanding some error or mistake in their judgements';[2] but they were none the less wrong. As time

[1] *The Savoy Declaration*, 1658, chap. 30, section 7.
[2] *Collected Works*, 1679, p. 119.

went by, and a generation of Friends grew up that had never known sacramental worship themselves, the dogma hardened. 'These rites,' said J. J. Gurney,[1] 'as they are now observed, are of precisely the same nature as the ceremonies of the ancient Jews. . . . Such Practices do not consist with that spiritual worship which is described as so distinguishing a feature of the dispensation of the gospel.'

What happens in a meeting for worship, beneath the silence? Attempts have been made in recent years to descry a rhythm or progress, corresponding in some way to the progress behind the ritual of the mass: but few Friends would accept the notion of any kind of structure. Early Friends struggled to express their sense that a change took place in the elements of their personality, elements hardened by habit and inertia, dissociated from each other by the experiences of daily life. Beneath the surface, they were trying to say, the parts fused and melted; and the only progress they would recognize was a sinking to this liquefying level. The imagery is, indeed, often 'liquid': 'in the melting and breaking of my spirit', 'his compassions, his tenderness, which have melted, overcome and changed my heart before him'. Thomas Story sustains the metaphor to bring out the sense that the individual discovers a kind of dynamic unity in which he and his fellow worshippers and the living God himself are involved:

> Not long after I had sat down among them, that heavenly and watery cloud overshadowing my mind brake into a sweet abounding shower of celestial rain, and the greatest part of the meeting was broken together, dissolved and comforted in the same divine and holy presence and influence of

[1] Observations on the Religious Peculiarities of the Society of Friends, 1824. (J. J. Gurney [1788-1847], a descendant of Robert Barclay, head of the family banking business, and active in support of Elizabeth Fry and of Buxton and Wilberforce in the anti-slavery campaign.)

the true, holy, heavenly Lord . . . And, as the many small springs and streams descending into a proper place and forming a river become more deep and weighty; even so thus meeting with a people gathered of the living God into a sense of the enjoyment of his divine and living presence, through that blessed and holy medium the Mind of Jesus Christ, the Son of God and Saviour of the world, I felt an increase of the same joy of the salvation of God. The meeting being ended, the Peace of God . . . remained as a holy canopy over my mind in a silence out of the reach of all words; and where no idea but the Word himself can be conceived.[1]

The worshipping attitude was expectant and receptive rather than deliberate and intentional. Time had to be spent, but not because 'exercises' had to be performed. This was no recitation of something learnt: it was rather a waiting to be uncovered, softened, broken, melted. William Penn sets out the contrast between a meeting of activity, of self-directed busy-ness, and one of waiting to be worked on:

When you come to your meetings . . . what do you do? Do you then gather together bodily only, and kindle a fire, compassing yourselves about with the sparks of your own kindling, and so please yourself and walk in the 'Light of your own fire, and in the sparks which you have kindled'? . . . Or rather, do you sit down in the True Silence, resting from your own Will and Workings, and waiting upon the Lord, with your minds fixed in that Light wherewith Christ has enlightened you, until the Lord breathes life into you, refresheth you, and prepares you, and your spirits and souls, to make you fit for his service, that you may offer unto him a pure and spiritual sacrifice?[2]

'To make you fit for his service.' These Friends would, in the end, describe their meetings for worship, not in traditional terms as the end to which all life tends, but as a

[1] *Journal*, 1747, pp. 32-3. (Thomas Story [1662-1742] of Kirklinton in Cumberland, traveller, naturalist, writer.)

[2] *A Tender Visitation*, *Works* 1771, p. 441.

means to the transmutation of all life. It is an argument that seems at first sight shockingly utilitarian: to 'use' worship, man's highest activity, as a means to 'life'. But this is the kind of rationality that Friends shrug off with impatience. True, 'worship' is man's highest activity; but 'worship' is not confined to 'meetings for worship'. We meet in silence to dig, to reach the depths where we ought to be living. Then we go back out of the silence to live on in the depths. The 'world' will slowly drag us up to the surface again: so we must meet again to find our way back; but the meeting remains a means to the living, the silent gathering for a time in preparation for a gathered dedication for all time.

> The silence is not a drowsy, unthinking state of the mind, but a sequestring or withdrawing of it from all visible objects and imaginations . . . praising the Invisible Omnipresent God, in his Light and Love; his Light gives wisdom and knowledge, and his Love gives power and strength, to run the ways of his commandments with delight . . . 'Such as get not forward in their spiritual journey when in meetings, it's certain they will go backwards when out of them.'[1]

'The Society of Friends,' says Evelyn Underhill, in some disappointment, 'has produced no great contemplative.' But Friends were not interested in contemplation, if by that is meant the mystical *via negativa* at its highest. They were concerned to be gathered up and used; and their meetings were places to be gathered in. There could be an argument here, over whether or not 'worship' is denigrated by such an attitude; but Friends would not join in: they would abide by their experience of a life that gains in unity and meaning precisely as 'worship' in silence leads out into 'worship' in love and service; and which is for the one and which for the other, they would not be prepared to say.

In practice, they defended their meetings as things of

[1] Epistle to the Q.M. of London and Middlesex, 1718, p. 14.

absolute necessity. When dissenting bodies were forbidden to hold services, Friends were virtually alone in refusing to go underground and meet in private. Their meeting houses were nailed up (sometimes with Friends inside them) but they continued to meet wherever they could, indoors or outdoors. Meetings were raided, and Friends hustled off to prison, but the remnant held fast. In Bristol, in 1681, when all dissenting meeting houses were pillaged and closed, Friends continued to worship in the entry to 'the Friars'. They were imprisoned, group after group of them, until in the end there were virtually no adult Friends at large, but the meeting was sustained by children, some of whom were themselves imprisoned or put in the stocks, or beaten 'with a faggot stick, which they bore patiently, the Lord no doubt supporting them. . . .'

The right to sit in silence was the costliest of their testimonies. But it was the dearest of them. They could not live without it.

V

Living in the Light

THE SEMINAL experience from which the Quaker movement sprang was George Fox's painful consciousness of the conflict between 'profession' and 'possession'. Men talked glibly enough about their religion, but outside their ritual and 'notions' they failed to live it: they were barren, and produced no fruit. Much of the Quaker challenge was therefore directed to the outcomes of Christian insight, the ethical consequences of the experience of encounter with the Light.

The challenge was incessant, beginning in the trivialities of personal conduct and developing in the course of time a more or less articulated policy in social and economic and international affairs. The trivialities were over-earnest: the refusal to remove hats, which stirred magistrates to such wrath; the use of 'thee' and 'thou' to strangers and superiors, which so annoyed the superiors; the plain dress, a frozen Puritan fashion; the sober speech, which must have made conversation with a Quaker strenuous. Much of this style came from Fox's own persuasion and example, and his vocation to unresting witness:

> Moreover, when the Lord sent me forth into the world, he forbade me to put off my hat to any, high or low; and I was required to 'thee' and 'thou' all men and women, without any respect to rich or poor, great or small. And as I travelled up and down I was not to bid people 'good morrow' or

> 'good evening', neither might I bow or scrape with my leg to any one. But oh!,

he continues, and we are not surprised,

> the rage that then was in the priests, magistrates, professors, and people of all sorts but especially in priests and professors![1]

Other Friends eagerly embraced the practices, not as a 'uniform' so much as an assertion of principle, essential to their own experience and message. Honesty in religion demanded honesty in speech and deed: they had to pierce through

> the husk and coatings of forms in which men's hearts and souls were wrapped up, and dragging them out from their lurking places into the open light of day.[2]

How, Friends would have asked, can you 'answer that of God' if you talk in the polite emptiness of convention? How be honest if you speak through a veil?

This Quaker style turned, almost inevitably, into a badge of membership, for the adoption of it soon came to represent the sign of commitment, the mark that 'something' had really 'happened' to work a change in the personality: the sign, as it were, of 'possession'. The danger that it would one day be no more than a mark of 'profession' was not at first apparent: for it was costly, a painful badge to wear. Thomas Ellwood (1639-1713)[3] describes how he came to it, after a meeting for worship 'like the clinching of a nail', leading to the point where he had to declare himself. He was filled with anxiety about 'how I should demean myself towards my acquaintance . . .

[1] *Journal*, p. 36.
[2] George Fox, *Guesses at Truth*, 1878 edn., p. 127.
[3] The friend of Milton, author of one of the most delightful Quaker journals.

> with whom I was wont to be jolly; whereas now I could not put off my hat, nor bow . . . nor use the corrupt language of *you* . . . but must keep to the plain and true language of *thou* and *thee* . . . But when they saw me stand still, not moving my cap, nor bowing my knee . . . they were amazed . . . At length the surgeon, a brisk young man . . . clapped his hand in a familiar way upon my shoulder, and smiling on me said, 'What, Tom, a Quaker?' To which I readily and cheerfully answered, 'Yes, a Quaker,' and as the words passed out of my mouth I felt a joy spring in my heart . . .[1]

It is understandable, this, that these trivial fruits of honesty should be tests of vocation, and be taken too seriously; but it was a pity, for they hardened into a habit which a second generation of Friends put on with eager scrupulousness, watching each other rigorously lest their dress and speech should become heathenish and gay. Margaret Fell, writing just before her death in 1702, voiced the view of the first generation, turning against Friends their own testimonies against 'the Jews' manner in outward things and ceremonies', complaining of these 'whimsical narrow imaginations', this 'silly poor gospel' that

> we must look at no colours, nor make anything that is changeable colours as the hills are . . . but we must all be in one dress and one colour . . . so much that poor Friends is mangled in their minds,

pleading that Friends should trust the free spirit they had met in Christ:

> Friends, we have one God, and one mediator betwixt God and man the man, Christ Jesus; let us keep to him or we are undone.[2]

Beneath this, there were larger issues. Honesty meant

[1] *The History of the Life of Thomas Ellwood*, 1714, p. 23.
[2] From a manuscript in the Library of Friends House, London.

more than plainness: it meant justice. And from the first, Friends were radical in their social criticism. It began with Fox's empirical attack on the abuses that stung him:

> About this time I was sorely exercised in going to their courts to cry for justice, and in speaking and writing to judges and justices to do justly, and in warning such as kept public houses for entertainment that they should not let people have more drink than would do them good, and in testifying against their wakes or feasts, their May-games sports, plays, and shows, . . . In fairs also, and in markets, I was made to declare against their deceitful merchandise and cheating and cozening, warning all to deal justly, to speak the truth, to let their 'yea' be 'yea' and their 'nay' be 'nay', and to do unto others as they would have others do unto them, and forewarning them of the great and terrible day of the Lord which would come upon them all. I was moved also to cry against all sorts of music, and against the mountebanks playing tricks on their stages, for they burdened the pure life and stirred up people's minds to vanity. I was much exercised, too, with schoolmasters and schoolmistresses, warning them to teach their children sobriety in the fear of the Lord, that they might not be nursed and trained up in lightness, vanity and wantonness. Likewise I was made to warn masters and mistresses, fathers and mothers in private families, to take care that their children and servants might be trained up in the fear of the Lord; and that they themselves should be therein examples and patterns of sobriety and virtue to them.[1]

This restless utterance did not at first go very deep, but it went *wide*, bringing the whole range of human activity under the charge of conscience. It was not to be long before a more coherent social theory was developed, partly by Fox, more systematically by Thomas Lawson and John Bellers. Fox, working as he always did from personal experience, addressed Parliament on the evils of the criminal law, the conditions of prison life, the death penalty for

[1] *Journal*, pp. 37-8.

petty crimes, the need for poor relief, which he proposed to finance by a violent mulcting of abbey lands and church and royal property. Thomas Lawson went further, proposing a labour exchange, 'a poor man's office', and a system of vocational education for the children of the poor: 'none to be put to service until they be first taught to spin, knit, sew or learn some trade by way of livelihood'.

The most sophisticated social theory of the time came from John Bellers, later to be described in *Das Kapital* as 'a veritable phenomenon in the history of political economy'. Much of his work is lost to us, through some unquakerish carelessness with his papers; but he is worthy of attention, as an example of what might have been, if Friends had let themselves take 'theory' seriously. He began, in true Quaker style, with prayer and the exploration of conscience, and the need for 'keeping atop of those things that cumber the mind'.

> He that keeps not a watch upon the thoughts of his heart is much out of his way; for, though he should imitate the best of forms, he is but of the outward court; it being impossible to worship God in the beauty of holiness with an irregular mind.[1]

This inward withdrawal made possible a tendering of the spirit in which the imagination could be set free to sense the human condition of another, while offering a man release from anxiety about his own:

> Make us, O Lord, what is right in Thy sight, suitable to the beings which Thou hast made us and the stations which Thou hast placed us in, that our tables nor nothing that we enjoy may become a snare unto us; but that the use and strength of all that we receive from Thy bountiful hand may be returned unto Thee.[2]

True social reform demanded first personal detachment and liberation from the temptations of the corrupt system. Only

[1] *Watch unto Prayer*, 1703. [2] Ib.

so would a man be free to judge and attack the structure. Bellers then ranged widely over the social and economic scene. At a time when the poor labourer was growing steadily poorer, and was acquiring a new serf-status,[1] Bellers argued that people were more valuable than land, and that 'people makes land valuable'. He proposed the foundation of 'Colleges of Industry', in which three hundred people would work for each other; and claimed that the poor had a right to livelihood, 'a comfortable living in the college to the industrious labourer being a rich man's debt and not their charity to them'.[2] The colleges would provide 'technical' education within a 'liberal' context: 'The hand employed brings profit, the reason in it makes wise, and the will subdued makes them good.' He pressed his plans as far as Parliament, pleading a passionate cause, fertile in economic criticism—of varying value, but always illuminated by high conscience, and inspired by an egalitarianism ahead of its time:

> How many distressed souls and helpless orphans lie in our streets as the dry bones in the valley, wanting to be gathered together by others' assistance before they can be united . . . They are capable of being saints on earth, and as angels in heaven. How much is owing to birth and education that hath made the difference between them and us? Was it our virtue or their vice that made the difference? Had we any capacity before we were born?

From this basis Bellers developed a series of schemes worthy of a modern government just before an election: a health scheme, with free hospitals, specializing in different diseases, medical research and medical schools in universities; a reform of the criminal law, with a rational scale of

[1] An Act of 1662 entitled a parish to remove any stranger back to his own parish unless he could guarantee that he would not claim relief.

[2] *Proposals for Raising a Colledge of Industry*, 1695.

punishments and radical prison reform; a proposal for unity between the sects on the basis of Christian action in politics; a small-scale reform of elections, involving the registration of voters; and a 'Parliament of Europe' with control of arms and a 'General Council' of the churches of Europe as a means of maintaining a unity of spirit across the frontiers of possible conflict.

Bellers was outside the true Quaker tradition, for he was a visionary with little practical skill. His immediate plans came to nothing: a 'workhouse' for distressed Friends in Bristol, soon to fail; a 'College' in London that dwindled away. But his visions were superb, and point our regret that the Quaker spirit was to become so exclusively practical. There were 'notions' here that were worthy of development.

The only solid achievement in economic affairs at this time lay in the demonstration that honest dealing was not only good morality, but was also sound practice. Quakers were soon known for their fixed prices and their refusal to haggle, setting 'the price at one word, which seemed offensive to many, who think they never buy cheap except they get abatement of the first price set upon them . . . to whom I answered they should not tempt any to break their words'.[1] Though this 'seemed offensive to many', it was good business sense in the end: 'Some Friends lost their custom at first . . . but afterwards people came to see . . . that they would not cozen or cheat them, and at last that they might send any child and be as well used as themselves, at any of their shops,[2] insomuch that the cry of all the professors and others was, "If we let these people alone they will take the trading of the nation out of our hands."[2]

The contrast between the fate of the social theory and this

[1] William Stout, a Lancaster ironmonger, *Autobiography*, p. 22.
[2] Fox, *Journal*, p. 169.

small but important item of practice illustrates the strength and weakness of the Quaker movement. Friends have never carried public opinion with them in their argument, even when the arguments were one day to be shown to be prophetic. They have been successful whenever they have been able to take a stand on their own, working out its consequences and paying its cost. The most notable example of this is the testimony against war, which began to look sensible, even to Christians, only when the bomb arrived to support it. But though the 'theory' has always been thought utopian, the vocation to personal pacifism has remained, remarkably consistent, and not infrequently costly, until the present day. For early Friends there were no theoretical problems involved at all. It was a simple response to the 'ethics of hope'. They felt themselves called to a level of life in which war had, almost overnight, disappeared from the field. 'I told (the Commonwealth Commissioners)', said Fox, when they wanted him to join the army,

> I lived in the virtue of that life and power that took away the occasion of all wars, and I knew from whence all wars did rise, from the lust . . . I told them I was come into the covenant of peace which was before wars and strifes were.[1]

'I was come into the covenant of peace.' Fox was not here arguing a pacifist 'case', deliberating over whether war was 'permissible' or not. He was describing a new order into which he had been called, a world seen in the Light, in which he had to live. The objection that the old order still existed, side by side with this—and that, indeed, the survival of the 'Children of Light' themselves depended on force of arms—was soon to be raised, and met by the full acceptance of the necessity of government, but the claim that some are called to live in the new order immediately.

[1] *Journal*, p. 65.

How, otherwise, could it come into being? Penington deals with this issue:

> I speak not this against any magistrate or peoples defending themselves against foreign invasions; or making use of the sword to suppress the violent and evil-doers within their borders—for this the present estate of things may and doth require, and a great blessing will attend the sword where it is borne uprightly to that end and its use will be honourable; and while there is need of a sword, the Lord will not suffer that government or those governors to want fitting instruments under them for the managing thereof, who wait on Him in His fear to have the edge of it rightly directed—but yet there is a better state, which the Lord hath already brought some into, and which nations are to expect and travel towards. Yea, it is far better to know the Lord to be the Defender, and to wait on Him daily, and see the need of His strength, wisdom and preservation, than to be never so strong and skilful in weapons of war.[1]

There was no intention in all this to declare the bearing of arms 'wrong'. Early Friends were not interested in ethical labels. What they were saying was that if Christ were taken seriously certain radical consequences must be accepted; and that this 'taking seriously' had to begin somewhere, in the actual lives of such people as 'saw'. Those who did not see the new order must live by what they did see: they had to be honest too, and the sword had to be 'borne uprightly'. But they ought, it was implied, to be grateful to those who had been summoned into the new order, and from whom would one day spread an insight that would eliminate war from the whole state.

The streak of realism about the needs of government was to be justified by events during the course of the 'holy experiment' in Pennsylvania. This began in 1681, with Charles II's grant to Penn of a tract of land in settlement of

[1] *Somewhat spoken to a Weighty Question concerning the Magistrates' Protection of the Innocent*, 1661.

a royal debt to Penn's father. Within limits set by the royal veto, Penn injected into the constitution and decisions of the new state a remarkable degree of the spirit of tolerance and trust. The famous treaty with the Indians—the only treaty, said Voltaire, 'never sworn to and never broken'; freedom of worship, a temperate and tender criminal code —all this showed a genuine spirit. But in the course of time the problem of defence, both of the colony itself and of the English crown, began to disturb the unity of the Quaker conscience. It was met, not with realist compromise, so much as with casuistical contrivance. When the Crown demanded its subsidy towards its wars in Europe, the Assembly in Pennsylvania voted £2,000, saying that they voted it for the Queen's use, and she must bear the responsibility of disposing of it. A few years later, they voted £4,000 for 'bread, beef, pork, flour, wheat, and other grains'; and later the formula 'for the King's use' was brought into play again.

While this 'political' device might have served for some time, the issue pressed harder when subsidies were called for to support the colonial governments direct, in their wars with the Indians. Quakers could deal with the Indians themselves, on a face-to-face basis; but they could neither avoid, nor join in, a war initiated by other governments. And in the end, they felt they could no longer govern. Friends outside the Assembly persuaded their leaders that a clear conscience was more important than good but imperfect government, and they withdrew.

This was in 1756, by which time Friends in both England and America had lost the urgent 'exploration' of conscience, and had settled in its place for the 'preservation' of conscience. It was the wrong road; and it was to be a long way back.

VI

Quietism

THE TESTING time for any movement for religious revival—indeed for any radical reform—is the second generation. When innovation becomes traditional, it loses its appeal to those of an innovating temper, and when a generation grows up to whom the 'new' ideas are old familiarities, the fire dies down. Friends were peculiarly susceptible to this decline, because the excitement of their early life had sprung from the experience of escape. They had suffered under a load of machinery; they had flung it away, and rejoiced in the freedom of spontaneous, inner-directed movement; and had walked cheerfully through the world in the sober gaiety of men liberated from tyranny.

But then their children grew up, to make a generation 'free', but not knowing what it was they were 'free from'. They were free, it is true, not to go to church, or take oaths, or repeat the creed, or be disciplined by a priest; but they had not felt, on their own pulse, the pressures from which they were released. What was there, in this inherited freedom, to be excited about?

And so they settled to the enjoyment and perfection of their peculiarity, seeking to make a pale in which they could live at peace with their own sensitive conscience. They were like a new monastic order, living within walls thrown up for the protection of true devotion, their life revolving round their own centre, their service of the world valuable and unselfish, but always stopping short of full involvement.

The capital difference between this period and what had gone before lay in the displacement of argument and dialogue by meditation. Early Friends were tireless in their challenge to the Church; and as long as they continued to argue, they were, perforce, taking the Christian tradition seriously. They rejected it, true, but they had to consider it. They had to find reasons for their own faith. Their message thus constituted a commentary on the tradition: it took account of the totality of Christian assertion. But early in the eighteenth century the argument died down, and Friends proceeded to the refinement of their own side of the case, untroubled by the necessity to meet the other side. The tradition was now not so much rejected as ignored. Theology was no longer challenged by the appeal to experience: it was no longer even understood.

Friends thus condemned themselves to a period of preoccupation with the inward life as the exclusive source of knowledge, and laid themselves peculiarly open to the Quietist influences abroad in Europe since the days of the Counter-Reformation, expressed in the writings of Miguel de Molino, Madage Guron, Fénélon and others. The Quaker form of the Quietist principle stemmed directly from the early warnings against the dangers of 'creatureliness' and the exercise of the human initiative in religious life. Busy thoughts, efforts at prayer, busy plans for action to be carried out in unaided human strength, had led to nothing but emptiness of spirit, anxiety and guilt. Then came the word of liberation, the simple call to 'wait in the Light', and the tension disappeared. Hence, it was assumed, the relaxed waiting was all that was required. Desire, even the desire for grace, or the desire to be of service, must be stilled, and the soul must let itself go, and enter directly into peace. 'The more absolute the self-renunciation,' said Fénélon, 'the deeper the peace.'[1] 'Gather thyself,' said John Churchman (1705-1775)[2] 'from all the cumbers of the world, and be thou weaned from the popularity, love and friendship thereof.'[3] From this level of peace, utterly untouched by the outward, would come the motive for action and the sign for its direction. Not only rational discourse, but even ordinary conversation, was hostile to this still withdrawal, as the Irish Quaker Richard Shackleton explained:

> My mind is too apt to be drawn out in these opportunities, from a still, quiet frame, into a flutter and commotion; and the affections of the creature to steal gradually into the room of the pure love of the Creator, who is ever jealous of his just right.[4]

'A state of emptiness, nothingness and abasement of self' he declares is the condition of mind in which the light can penetrate.

The first impact of this attitude was on the meeting for worship, in which Friends now set guards upon themselves to make certain that they brought nothing of the 'creaturely' or offered in spoken ministry nothing of their own thoughts. The ministry of the first period might be described as 'persons ministering': the whole person, drawn up to a new level but still the person, with all his intellectual powers active, his experience and interpretation of life, his sufferings and struggles given point, brought to a coherent view 'in the Light'. Quietist ministry was believed rather to be a direct word from God, 'given' from 'out there' to an instrument who served as mouthpiece without any con-

[1] *Spiritual Letters*, Letter XXVIII.
[2] Born in Pennsylvania, a friend of John Woolman.
[3] *Journal*, p. 104, 1748.
[4] Memoirs and Letters of Richard and Elizabeth Shackleton, 1882, p. 10.

tribution from his own thought and life. Richard Shackleton describes a meeting rich in ministry as being 'favoured' by 'instrumental help' and reflects on how 'precious it is for . . . human nature to be influenced by a supernatural power'. And when one of these 'instruments' found himself without a word to offer, he was puzzled and bewildered at the failure of the divine support, but not at all inclined to look for the cause of the failure in his own personal equipment. Job Scott,[1] travelling in Pennsylvania and New Jersey, describes such an experience:

> On the 10th, I had a meeting at Fair Hill; I was silent there.
> Fourth day, 11th, had a meeting at Germantown, in which my lot was silence.
> Fifth day, 12th, attended the Youths' General Meeting at Byberry, and suffered still in silence, feeling myself as a stranger, a pilgrim on the earth; and in the depth of my distress, I said in my heart, Lord, why hast thou thus forsaken me? . . . Thus . . . I bemoaned my desolate condition, and spread my case before the Lord my God with tears, but all in a good degree of resignation: and after a little space, being fully satisfied all would work for good, I was made willing to be as poor, empty and blind as the Lord would have me to be, and all centred in this: 'Not my will, but Thine be done.'[2]

What we have here is a concentration on a half-truth: that 'being busy' is not enough. The creative artist knows this is true, when his conscious effort and deliberate disposal of his material fails to fuse, and he must wait, trusting and relaxed, for 'something to happen' beneath the level of consciousness. The farmer knows it when he waits to let the seed grow. We all know it when we 'sleep on a problem'. But the other half-truth, that artist and farmer and we ourselves dare not forget, is that 'being *unbusy*' is not enough.

[1] Born in Rhode Island, 1751.
[2] *Journal*, p. 206.

The farmer, after all, has to plough and sow, though the seed is given and a mystery he must handle with awe.

The result of the false half of this half-truth was a tendency towards a certain measure of irresponsibility. It was, after all, a deprivation for the Friends who had travelled into meeting to 'hear' Job Scott that they should not hear him at all, and that he should learn to be 'poor, empty and blind' at their expense. And while this danger must be set against the danger it was meant to avoid—of smooth, well-prepared utterance from the wrong level of the personality, diverting but uncreative—the whole effort of the Society was now set so firmly in the wrong direction that they began to neglect the effort on which progress must depend. A Quaker doctor committed to his journal his agonized leadings away from medicine, where surely his responsibility lay, to introspection and clearness of conscience: 'Do less in medicine and nature, saith the Lord, and more in spirituals . . . Wean me, O Lord, from the world and from the specious glitterings of natural science.' Beware of politics, Friends began to say to each other, in the not unfounded suspicion that here was an area in which the conscience was often likely to be unclear. Beware of working too hard, they went on, of making too much money, of letting business 'cumber the mind'. And again they were half right. But again they were half wrong.

The Quietist tendency was, in a sense, an over-particular search for peace of mind. The witness of the Light, it was believed, would be recognized by the purely inward sign of harmonious personal experience: when the mind and heart were free of conflict and doubt, when the inner life rose up pure to meet the Light, then was the Light known. What other men said, whether in tradition, book, or word, was irrelevant: all that mattered was the immediate sense of an immediate word.

They concentrated their attention, in brief, on the here-and-now, the moment in which they believed God spoke directly to their condition. But they overlooked the way in which their 'condition' would affect their powers of hearing. They forgot the extent to which previous learning would shape their consciousness, make them ready to hear one message but deaf to another. They forgot, indeed, as they ignored the broader Christian tradition, and the generalizing and critical function of theology, that their own tradition was now in command of their personalities, and that a lack of critical debate spelt danger to personal growth.

VII

Guarding the Light

WE HAVE seen how the first Friends designed a minimal structure for the maintenance of community and the effective presentation of their message; and that this structure provided for a face-to-face encounter between men who had something to bring in the excitement of their meeting with the Light. The primary organizational problem at that time was to contain enthusiasm; and this was solved by a system of meetings that enabled Friends to talk to each other, or to sit together in a silence that bound them together. Their characteristic lines of activity ran out, almost without thought or intention, from the abounding life flowing between them and through them. By the next century the problem was reversed. Now the life was low, and what was needed was a structure that could be set to work in the opposite direction: to promote activity instead of curbing it, to raise zeal instead of controlling it. But the machine would not go into reverse. Instruments designed for control, necessary and beneficent as long as there was a powerful urge to be controlled, became ineffective when they worked on the Quietist temper. As long as Friends were looking outwards, their frequent meetings were a source of power. As soon as they turned inwards, they produced monotony of tone and temper, and a pedantry over organization.

The three main problems to which Friends turned their

attention were membership, decision-taking, and conduct. Who *were* Friends, now that they had lost hope of winning the whole Church to their trust in the Light? How were they to be organized, so as to preserve the liberty of the Light in a settled structure? And how were those Friends to be dealt with who fell away from the standard of Christian conduct to which the Society was committed? In any other church the answer to these questions was tolerably clear. The baptized and communicant were members. The priest or minister exercised at least the initiative and executive power of decision, with varying degrees of assistance from leading laymen. And the priest or minister similarly exercised the pastoral responsibility, both in its positive, hortatory aspect and in its negative, disciplinary aspect. But Friends were committed to the denial of baptism, communion and priesthood. What substitute could be provided?

It became necessary to define the membership when the practice of supporting Friends in prison became an established habit of supporting all Friends in need. As long as persecution was a reality, there was little need to be exact about membership: suffering was its own badge. But when emergency relief had turned into a continuing welfare fund, it became necessary to know who were Friends and who were not; and in 1737 London Yearly Meeting defined membership, to include 'the wife and children of a member, not only during his life, but after his decease'. There are two oddities here. The definition of membership was designed to mark out the actual situation: to guard against an influx of new members coming in for the wrong reason. And being so designed, it became, in a way that baptism or other ceremonial is not, almost a disincentive to joining the Society. The open group of the early days, eagerly drawing in people who found themselves in sympathy with it, became at once crystallized, 'listed', with a border to be crossed. Further, the automatic membership, for life, of 'wife and children', meant that the Society now contained many members who had not passed through the liberating experience which most early Friends had shared in some degree. While all early Friends had 'come in', there were now to be many members who had done nothing except not 'go out'. Among these would be many who were not, at first hand, aware of what the Society was all about; and would inevitably confront the leadership with problems of a new kind.

But who were the leaders? Fox had created a structure which raised no barriers to initiative, and was open to all Friends who had anything to bring. The early practice of making Monthly Meeting 'select', by invitation from those Friends who were most 'seasoned' and 'active', put a further emphasis on initiative. So long as Friends *were* active, loving and imaginative, this rhythm between the 'meeting-of-all' and the 'nurture-by-the-few' represented the most dynamic possible way of dealing with the facts of human nature. But when activity began to fail, the test of a 'seasoned' Friend became the test of orthodoxy, and often, inevitably, of extremity in orthodoxy. Slowly the view of leadership changed from 'persons of power' to 'persons of status', from the concentration of resources to the defence of settled positions. A minute of London Yearly Meeting in 1676 ran:

> All the faithful men and women in every county and city and nation, whose faith stands in the power of God, the Gospel of Christ, and have received the Gospel and are in possession of this Gospel—they have a right to the power of the Meeting.

By 1776, the 'power of the Meeting' was firmly settled in the hands of men with labels.

The labels were 'minister', 'elder' and 'overseer'. 'Ministers' were those Friends of insight and, perhaps, fluency, whose contributions to meetings for worship were consistently well received. They were not appointed, but recorded: they had to prove themselves first. It is an important distinction, for it guarded the right of all Friends to offer ministry, while it provided a measure of recognition of those who were consistently acceptable. 'Elders' were Friends of 'weight' but not fluency, representing the receptive members of the meeting, with the task of advising and encouraging ministers or warning and discouraging them. In 1727 London Yearly Meeting called for them to be set up in all meetings:

> This Meeting desires all Monthly Meetings to appoint serious, discreet and judicious Friends, who are not Ministers, tenderly to Encourage and help young Ministers, and advise others as they shall in the wisdom of God see occasion: and that where there are meetings of Ministering Friends, such Friends so chosen be admitted as members of such Meetings of Ministers, and Act therein for the good purposes aforesaid.[1]

During the next fifty years it became clear that there were two different pastoral tasks. In addition to this nurture of ministry, there was need for the control of conduct. In 1789 Yearly Meeting determined that all meetings should distinguish between the two tasks by appointing both Elders and Overseers. Elders became the more important, for they slipped into the position of being the trustees of sound doctrine, not only encouraging young Ministers but

> keeping all ministers to the truth and seeing that none pretend to be wise above what is written, or in a pretended wisdom go about to explain the things of God in man's wisdom.[2]

[1] Y.M. Minutes, vol. vi, p. 461.
[2] Epistles of London Yearly Meeting, vol. i, p. 181.

As any magistrate knows, silence, a grave demeanour, and the right to pass judgement on others are powerful elements in the creation of an impressive image; and during the late eighteenth and early nineteenth centuries the image of the Quaker Elder was as awful as any possessed by a priest of the middle ages. They were the silent servants of the invisible Quaker altar. They acquired, says Rufus Jones (1863-1948),[1]

> the power to sit through the longest meetings without stirring or moving. They never seemed to look at anything and yet they saw everything that happened. If anybody fell asleep they knew it . . . They seemed unmoved as the desert sphinx while some Minister was preaching and no change of facial muscle betrayed in the least their approval or disapproval, but if the Minister made the slightest slip in quoting Scripture, or if he deviated from 'truth', or if his garb, or voice, or manner revealed that he was not 'seasoned' or 'savoury' or 'in the life', *he* would know it himself before he got home . . . They were meek and gentle to look upon, but somehow they acquired an extraordinary mastery over the membership. What they meditated in silence sooner or later became a fact . . . They wove the dead past into the living present and kept the 'truth' as near as possible unaltered.[2]

In the course of time their task became codified in a collection of Advices for Ministers and Elders, the 1783 version of which included injunctions 'against undue and restless behaviour under the ministry of any Friend', against 'unnecessary preambles . . . and unbecoming tones, sounds and gestures and all affectation, which are not agreeable to Christian gravity', against 'men and women travelling as companions in service, to avoid all occasions of offence thereby', against ostentatious living in their own homes or 'burthensome visits to others', and against indifference to

[1] Professor of Philosophy, Haverford College, Pennsylvania.
[2] *The Later Periods of Quakerism*, London, 1921, vol. i, p. 126-7.

others 'that ministering Friends be careful not to hurt one another's service in publick meetings, but every one have a tender regard for others; that nothing be offered with a view to popularity, but in humility, and the fear of the Lord. . . . And lastly, As prayer and supplication to God is an essential part of his worship, it must be performed in spirit and in truth, with a right understanding seasoned with grace. Therefore let Ministers be careful how and what they offer in prayer, avoiding many words and repetitions, and not to run from supplication into declaration, as though the Lord wanted information . . . neither let prayer be in a formal and customary way, to conclude a meeting, without an awful sense of divine assistance attending the mind.'[1]

It is an illuminating document, both for its statement of its narrow but admirable ideal, and its frank admissions of the ways in which the practice fell short: the eagerness and tactlessness of Ministers, the desire to make an impression, the temptation to let words run away from the Word in the depths. Friends were not to realize for generations the extent to which this anti-authoritarian society had come to depend on authority; yet today, looking back, we can both see the irony of the shift, and appreciate the necessity for it. Without the life that is above the law, there must always be the law; and without their unintended realism in the acceptance of this principle eighteenth-century Friends would almost certainly have dwindled into nothing. They hedged their dim little light about, but in a curious way they preserved it against the time when they should meet the Light again in open day.

The appointment of Overseers demonstrated the same truth in the same ambivalent form. They, too, represented realism breaking in on principle. It had been assumed that the pastoral task of controlling the conduct of the members

[1] Extracts from Minutes and Advices of London Y.M., 1793, p. 149.

of the Meeting was vested in the group as a whole. whose deep unity was regarded as expressing the mind of Christ. But the groups often failed to reach this level of unity, and it became necessary in practice to appoint particular Friends to act, discreetly and tenderly, on behalf of the Meeting. Like Elders and Ministers, Overseers were aided by a summary guide, in the shape of General Advices, within the broad lines of which Overseers gave individual counsel or warning. These Advices, which originated in the early days, were revised, and are still revised, in the light of current problems and temper. The version current in 1800 ran as follows:

> Friends are advised
>
> 1 To observe due moderation in the furniture of their houses; and to avoid superfluity in their manner of living.
>
> 2 To attend to the limitations of truth in their trade, and other outward concerns.
>
> 3 To be careful to place out children, of all degrees, amongst those friends whose care and example will be most likely to conduce to their safety; to prefer such servants and apprentices as are members of our Society; and not to demand exorbitant apprentice-fees . . .
>
> 4 To endeavour to make way for their servants to attend meetings, and to encourage them therein.
>
> 5 To guard carefully against the introduction of pernicious books into their families.
>
> 6 To make their wills, and settle their outward affairs, in time of health.
>
> 7 To refrain from being concerned in lotteries: which this meeting considers as a species of gambling.
>
> 8 Finally, it is recommended that all friends watch over one another for good; that when occasion of uneasiness first appear in any, they may be treated with in privacy and

> tenderness, before the matter be communicated to another. Thus the hands of those concerned in the further exercise of the discipline will not be weakened by a consciousness of their having themselves departed from the true order of the gospel. And friends everywhere are advised to endeavour to maintain the 'unity of the spirit in the bond of peace'.[1]

It is an unexciting view of the Christian life, this: solid furniture, well-managed servants, a respectable bookshelf, a well-made will, and no gambling—it all seems a far cry from the tendering of spirit and outgoing love that were the marks of the early Society. And when the 'Queries' were asked and called for a formal answer, it became plain that the life of the Society was at a low ebb.

It was a sign of decay that the Queries had to be 'answered' at all. The secret of the early ethic was its reliance on the love of persons, knowing each other, sustaining each other, sensitively aware of each other's condition, all at a deeper level than could be reached through the weighing of acts and accounting in words. When now it began to seem that accounting in words was possible, when Friends began to assume that they could report on themselves in round terms, the springs of life were being neglected. A list used in 1760 included the following:

> Are the meetings for worship and discipline duly attended and do Friends avoid all unbecoming behaviour therein?
>
> Are Friends careful to avoid all vain sports, places of diversion, gaming, and all unnecessary frequenting of ale-houses or taverns, excess in drinking, and intemperance of every kind?
>
> Is early care taken to advise and deal with such as appear inclinable to marry contrary to the rules of our Society?[2]

[1] *Extracts*, 2nd edition, 1802.

[2] 'Nearly five thousand persons had been disowned from the Society in the preceding half century for marrying contrary to the rule of discipline.' Rufus Jones, on the year 1859, when the rule was relaxed. *The Later Periods of Quakerism*, 1921, p. 951.

> And do no Friends remove from or into your Monthly . . . Meetings without certificates?
>
> Do you keep a record of your Monthly Meetings of the prosecutions and sufferings of your respective members? and have you a record of your meeting-houses and burial-grounds, &c.? . . .

When meetings spend their time together finding the answers to these questions, it may be suspected that they begin to neglect the duty of digging about the roots of the tree.

By 1800 the Society of Friends had become a rigid institution, subject to the very institutional faults against which early Friends had carried out their costly struggle; and it might seem as if the Quaker task was finished. But there were two ways in which this negative period had its value in the total exploration of Christian experience, ways that 'pure' Quakerism neglected, and later Quakerism discovered it could not do without. Institutionalism and tradition were harmful, said early Friends, because they stood in the way of the pure life; but this, the eighteenth-century Society was to demonstrate, was not the whole story. While freedom from 'the Law' was necessary for those who could see beyond it, the Law was necessary for those who could not see. The Christian life, so long as it is lived by men and not angels, remains a life of tension between authority and freedom: between the outward 'lesson' and the inward learning. Insight is insight into a situation, not a pure creative act inwardly determined. This capital principle emerges more clearly from the eighteenth-century experience than it does from the excitement and liberation of what went before; and it may be that one of the most important 'lessons of Quakerism' is the one we learn from the time when Friends, judged by their own pure doctrine, were lost.

At the same time, the period threw up one genius who flowered both 'through' and 'despite' the tradition in which he was nurtured. John Woolman was a native of New Jersey, whose journal still stands as the purest and sweetest flowering of the Quaker spirit. He tells us little about the quiet, stable environment in which he grew up, but he makes plain that he spent some years in the exercise of his conscience in the typical young man's conflict between the moral pressures around him and the desire for gaiety and satisfaction.

> Having attained the age of Sixteen, I began to love wanton company; and though I was preserved from profane language or Scandalous conduct, still I perceived a plant in me which produced much wild Grapes.[1]

He applied the standard remedy: withdrawal.

> I learned this: That, if I would live in the Life which the Faithful servants of God lived in, I must not go into company as heretofore in my own Will; but all the cravings of Sense must be governed by a Divine principle.[2]

He remained faithful in his attendance at Meeting, and suffered the common experience of offering ministry from the wrong level, and being filled with guilt:

> One day . . . I stood up, and said some words in a meeting; but not keeping close to the Divine opening, I said more than was required of me; and I was afflicted in mind some weeks, without any light or comfort.[3]

Then, when he had accepted his discipline, he was released:

> Feeling the spring of Divine Love opened, and a Concern to Speak, I said a few Words in a meeting, in which I found peace; this I believe was about six weeks from the first time.

[1] *The Journal of John Woolman*, ed. A. M. Gummere, 1922, N.Y. and London, p. 153.
[2] Ib., p. 156. [3] Ib., p. 159.

In these introspective exercises, and in similar scrutiny of his own responsibility for disorderly conduct around him, Woolman was engaged on a 'critique of pure conscience' which was to serve him well in greater things.

They began in a small way, when his employer, a shopkeeper, asked him to write out a bill of sale for a woman slave. 'The Thing was sudden', and he convinced himself that he ought to comply; but from this 'stop' in his mind he began to look afresh at the institution of slavery. On the next occasion he refused to act, and said why; and this began a long struggle; first against the Quakers who owned slaves, and finally against the entire system. He was led outwards, as early Friends had argued would happen, from the particular to the general; and from the basic hunch, that 'the Practice was not right', he ranged out to the facts about the trade in flesh, from its base in Africa, the disrupted home life and broken relationships, though the tragic losses on the voyage to the life the slave was doomed to in America. This was how the Quaker conscience was meant to work: not to 'take up a cause', but to value persons, and to explore from the particular case of suffering the whole network of prejudice, habit and plain evil in which the suffering became inevitable. This was, too, what Quakers understood to be the consequences of living in the Light: for Woolman was led above the standards of his time in a fresh vision of the meaning of personality. Here was more than the well-trained conscience, discriminating in the familiar. It was a moral innovation.

The same spirit is seen in Woolman's dealings with the Indians, at a time when other settlers were still hostile, living on stolen land, and ready to go to war at the least ruffling of the waters. Woolman was moved to travel in Indian territory, not to preach or persuade, but to enter into their condition: 'that I might feel and understand their life, and the spirit they live in, if haply I might receive some instruction from them, or they be in any degree helped forward by my following the leadings of Truth amongst them'. The story of his journey is a classic of inner-directed enterprise, in which the dangers that threatened set up a conflict, not of fear, but of doubt whether he was advancing in pure obedience or in a spirit of bravado.

> In this conflict of Spirit there were great Searchings of Heart . . . that no motion might in the least degree be attended to but that of the pure Spirit of Truth.[1]

Woolman was a perfect exemplar of Quaker empiricism. He was sufficiently well-informed about slavery to meet the crude arguments of its defenders, but he was never near a fully developed scheme for the solution of the problem. He never worked out the long-term implications of his attitude to the Indians. He wore simple, undyed clothes as a testimony against luxury, but had no coherent economic theory. Yet if the Quaker contribution was the awakening of conscience, he was its most restless and disturbing exponent. On his last journey, to England and to his death, he travelled in the squalor of steerage, and rejoiced because doing so exposed him to a knowledge of the conditions of the crew. In England he refused to ride in stage-coaches, but walked through the land, asking awkward questions about wages and the cost of necessities, and setting it all down in his journal with the comment, 'May those who have abundance lay these things to heart.' In his last words, penned on his death-bed, he lamented the condition of Friends themselves, not for any wickedness, but because the gradual turning of their attention to trade and comfort and respectability had weakened their vision : 'a dimness of sight came over many'.

The main body of the Society was, indeed, busy with

[1] Ib., p. 250.

lesser things: bearing their testimonies, standing firm, but making no significant advances. They were quietly fighting against the payment of tithes and church rates, as an assertion of the right of conscience and of their concept of a free ministry of the gospel. There were some imprisonments, and some deaths in prison, but in general this was a financial struggle in which Friends suffered distraints beyond the value of the tithes—three-quarters of a million pounds being distrained between 1730 and 1830. They continued to testify against bearing arms. In the Irish rebellion of 1789 they threw their undefended homes open to the hunted and wounded victims of battle. They testified against oaths until Parliament granted them the right to affirm. They maintained their austere dress and manner, the badge of their peculiarity. They continued to guard their little light from the winds of the world.

These 'testimonies' were of varying value, and even the best of them come under judgement from the radical Quaker principle. Yet in a curious way they served the Society well in these days when the life was low. They protected it and hedged it and helped in its survival. The Society was in these days a 'holy club' rather than a 'holy experiment'; but it was marked by a certain undeniable holiness.

There were, inevitably, defaulters. Some members were too accommodating about tithes. Some members, called to the militia, 'failed in the maintenance of our Christian Testimony against Warrs and fightings by joyning with others to hire Substitutes'.[1] Even Yearly Meeting itself sent an adulatory address to George II on the failure of the rebellion of '45, rejoicing in 'this signal instance of divine favour'.

But the total achievement, lacking as it is in excitement, is not to be despised. Here was a group of people who had

[1] Minutes of London Yearly Meeting, vol. xii, p. 105.

lost touch with their sources of creative life, who yet maintained in faithfulness a habit, a way of living, that carried the challenge of conscience. They had the strength to resist the culture around them; and it will always be a mark of a Christian community that it resists the culture. They held their own members open to each other; and this, too, is a mark of a living church. And they maintained at the centre of their life and activity a place of worship in which there was no longer richness and movement, but in which there never failed to be awe and a stern and challenging, but genuine, love. Without these things they must have disappeared. With them, they survived into a time when new winds would shake them and set them astir again.

VIII

Quakerism at Work

IN THE end the Society of Friends was saved by its institutions, by the half-truth that their message overlooked. Friends settled down to operate the machine, with such devotion that in time they began to recover the adventurous spirit that had shaped it. Genuine commitment to the machinery carried with it commitment to the attitudes it was meant to express. Commitment to the awful silence carried with it an assumption—and in this sphere assumptions may be more powerful than a delicately held set of concepts—that God existed and was to be met; that man was meant to meet him; that the meeting began in honest looking. And when a man had worked on this assumption for three or four hours, he was likely to be the more ready to approach his other experiences on the same assumptions; to expect the beyond-in-the-midst, to dig about the other events of his life, looking for meaning. Similarly, the interdependence of the silence, the sense that the worshippers needed each others' struggle, involved a belief in a God of love, a God whose life was in some way shared by men-in-society. And four hours of being held in this assumption made a man ready to meet other men with something of the same 'feeling sense'. So also with the tension in action : initiative and responsibility, assertion and submission, action based on 'the truth' as 'I see it' controlled by judgement based on 'the truth as they see it', provided that both judgements are honestly based on 'truth as we see it' : here is a habit of mind that can be transferred constructively to the ordinary problems of living, and will make anyone more purposeful and more effective in his approach to them.

They were 'saved' in the sense that they were held fast in the belief that it was a man's business to plumb the depths of his personality, to reach—what can we say?—the Light? God? Reality? the eternal Other? ground of ultimate concern? the ground of being? The eighteenth-century Friend would have been impatient with the attempt to say what it was he met: something 'real', he would have insisted, but something too deep for words. They were held too by the belief that other men could be met at this depth, and could be helped to find their own depth; and thus they carried out into their ordinary life a readiness, not to take men's responsibility from them, but to enable them to achieve it for themselves. Here, then, are the two dominant motives of the Quaker life: conscience, ranging through the whole of life and reaching down to the depths below categories and concepts, to the ultimately personal; and altruism, the assertion of the other in his ultimately personal. These two habits of mind were to determine their chief contribution as they earned their living and looked out for occasion to give what they could.

They lay, for example, behind the Quaker achievement in trade and industry. We have already seen that 'honesty' proved the 'best policy'; and now the questioning, humble and open mind, and the sense of responsibility for others were to be good policy too. Friends were, indeed, fortunately placed for success in trade. It was not the activity of the gentleman, but Friends did not believe in gentlemen, and were not ashamed to work. It called for intelligence and adventurous thought, and here Friends were at an advantage over the established church, for they were unable to send their sons to Oxford and Cambridge, so their best minds were free for unscholarly, practical pursuits. Furthermore, Friends were sober and earnest, believing that work was better than play. And beneath all this was the digging spirit, looking for the 'truth' of a matter, with the obstinate grasping at essentials that 'clears the mind of cant'. So they were notable in technical innovation and in building up new structures of human relationships that have left behind an indelible Quaker mark on our industrial system. The names of Cadbury, Fry, Rowntree, Bryant and May, Huntley and Palmer, Allen and Hanbury, Barclay and Lloyd remain as landmarks of their effort and skill. They were to be pioneers in the railway system. William Beck can hardly contain his pride on this theme:

> Friend Edward Pease was the first to discover, and the most persistent in fostering the railway genius of a George Stephenson . . . It was Friend Ellis of Leicester who started the now great Midland . . . In the matter of rails, Friend Ransome devised the best form of chair for holding them, and Charles May the compressed oak trenails that pin them to the ties . . . It was Friend Ellis who devised the present effective system of railway tickets, and likewise invented the machine in general use for stamping them; and it is Friend Bradshaw who still enlightens the public as to train movements by his time tables.[1]

As we read this, the dark thought may cross our minds that Christianity is not about machines for stamping railway tickets; but it is, among other things, about taking things and persons seriously; and this kind of seriousness was the direct outcome of a deeper seriousness. In the same way, Christianity is not about making money: but it *is* about the kind of integrity in industry that carries with it, embarrassingly, financial success.

[1] William Beck, *The Friends: Who They Are—What They Have Done*, 1897, pp. 227-30.

Another area into which the Quaker habit of mind moved easily was the study of science. The names are here less well known, apart from Lister, Dalton, and, in this century, Eddington. But since the seventeenth century the Royal Society has never been without Quakers among its Fellows; and ordinary Friends have always found the world of things congenial, particularly such quiet aspects of it as natural history and mathematics, or such humane disciplines as medicine. Thus, very early Friends became botanists, and made clocks and navigational aids; and Robert Barclay commends this kind of endeavour as not 'wholly superfluous' and unlikely to 'lead the mind into lust, vanity and wantonness, innocent diversions which may sufficiently serve for relaxation of the mind such as . . . to follow after gardening, use geometrical and mathematical experiments, and such other things of this nature'.

The same principle appears in Quaker thought about education. The first generation had reacted, as Bacon and Locke reacted, against the verbalism and irrelevance of the curriculum of the seventeenth century. Penn voices the characteristic criticism:

> We are in pain to make them scholars but not men, to talk rather than to know . . .
>
> The first thing obvious to children is what is sensible, and that we make no part of their rudiments.
>
> We press their memory too soon, and puzzle, strain and load them with words and rules, to know grammar and rhetoric and a strange tongue or two, that it is ten to one may never be useful to them, leaving their natural genius to mechanical and physical or natural knowledge uncultivated and neglected, which would be of exceeding use and pleasure to them through the whole course of their life.
>
> Children had rather be making of tools and instruments of play, shaping, drawing, framing, and building, etc., than getting some rules of propriety of speech by heart; and those also would follow with more judgement and less trouble and time.

> It were happy if we studied nature more in natural things, and acted according to nature, whose rules are few, plain and most reasonable.[1]

These anticipations of Froebel were to be long in being realized, and when the first Quaker boarding school was opened at Ackworth in 1779 it was conventional enough. But the Quaker principle was there; and though Friends themselves never worked it out in systematic practice, they touched, from time to time, the right chords. Lindley Murray's[2] famous English Grammar was an early attempt at escaping from the classics, with their aristocratic connexions, into the vernacular. Joseph Lancaster (1778-1838) was working from principle in his experiments in a cheap, popular education as did, in another sphere, the Adult School Movement. In education at various levels, Friends were seeking to reach the depths of human life, and to uncover human potential.

They were trying to do the same in their efforts at prison reform. Elizabeth Fry's work was directed towards those in whom 'that of God' was hard to recognize: the poor of her own neighbourhood, and then the women prisoners in Newgate, to all appearance mere animal, but touched by something in Elizabeth Fry's approach:

> I heard weeping, and I thought they appeared much tendered; a very solemn quiet was observed; it was a striking scene, the poor people on their knees around, in their deplorable conditions.[3]

Then she ranged more widely, creating a society for the reform of prisons and the criminal law; giving evidence before a Commons committee; advancing a plea for constructive occupation:

[1] Some Fruits of Solitude, 1693.

[2] Born in Pennsylvania, 1745, at first a barrister in New York, later in England, a prolific writer of school books. The famous *English Grammar* was published in 1795.

[3] *Memoirs*, vol. i, p. 225.

> We may instruct as we will, but if we allow them their time, and they have nothing to do, they naturally must return to their evil passions.[1]

Then on further, to the publication of reports, and a wide-ranging interest in all aspects of the treatment of criminals: the conditions on transports to New South Wales, conditions on arrival, the foundation of day-nurseries, and of societies to aid discharged prisoners—all of it soundly based on restless fact-finding and a powerful, unsentimental hope.

A similar story, in the same classic Quaker mode, was that of William Tuke's[2] revolutionary treatment of the insane. At a time when watching the antics of the inmates of Bedlam was still legitimate entertainment, and when even George III was chained during his bouts of madness, William Tuke set his patients free. He founded 'The Retreat' in York, in 1796, and there replaced constraint by courageous kindliness and reassurance. Patients were set to work —'occupational therapy' was in these days a characteristic Quaker prescription both for the sick and the healthy. They were told that their cure depended largely on their own efforts; and when they grew violent William Tuke would sit quietly beside them, persuasive and comforting. In the Retreat the first attempts were made at the classification of mental diseases, opening the way to later scientific studies.

And there are other stories: Joseph Sturge (1793-1859) and J. J. Gurney in the campaign for the emancipation of slaves, leading and focusing Quaker opinion in Wilberforce's larger effort. Or the variegated activity of William Allen (1778-1843), who wrote in his youthful diary,

[1] *Memoirs*, vol. i, p. 322.

[2] William Tuke (1732-1822), tea and coffee merchant in York. His son, grandson and great-grandson all won an entry in the Dictionary of National Biography for philanthropy and innovation in mental treatment.

> Indulged the flesh too much this morning by lying in bed till eight o'clock. Oh, my lightness and chaffiness! Lord, strengthen me to oppose it.[1]

But he became a competent, all-round scientist and linguist, a Fellow of the Royal Society, a pioneer in pharmaceutics and a social reformer, ranging from Spitalfields to New Lanark, a campaigner against capital punishment and a 'peace ambassador' through Europe. Or the story could be told of William E. Forster (1818-1886), 'disowned' by the Society for marrying a non-Friend (Matthew Arnold's sister) but carrying the fruits of his Quaker upbringing into the struggle for the Education Act of 1870.

So we could run on with the tale: the same questioning of the condition of the people, the same hope of the people, the same resolute active service. It would not be a tale of unique quality, for the spirit of philanthropy was abroad: the nineteenth century called for it, and there were others, besides Quakers, to respond. What matters is that they did respond, these exclusive Quakers. They set up their religious and moral hedge round themselves, but within the hedge they developed a concern for others that redeemed, in the end, the pedantry of their belief and practice. The work itself was narrower than it should have been, by the withdrawal from politics, by the reluctance to engage in the Christian mission, by the persistent failure to push their experiment and adventure into the field of theory. What might have emerged from a combination of Elizabeth Fry and John Bellers!

But within these limits, these Friends, for all their inward turning, were outward feeling and outward working. They were not easy to enlist in the service of 'causes': but they were deeply sensitive to situations in which they could serve, and peculiar though they were, they remained in

[1] *Life*, vol. i, p. 4.

touch, at a deep level of the personality, with the realities around them. They were living out a kind of holy worldliness; and if the holiness was a little monotonous, and the worldliness a little mixed with the less than holy, there was a certain 'wholeness' about it. There was more of habit and custom in this Quakerism than early Friends could have tolerated; but the habits were creative of personality: they produced a type of character that could respond to vocation.

IX

Shaking Free

THE HUNDRED years from 1850 saw the loosening of the iron bonds of the Quaker habit, a slow, unspectacular 'modernizing' of the Society, and its permeation by a spirit of adaptability that has restored to this peculiar people something of its early openness. Friends had been living, since their second generation, in a curious dualism, moving between the 'still centre' and the shifting frontier, between the guarded life within the hedge and the unwrapped territory of industry, and social reform. They were saved, when the saving came, by the movement from one to the other, the outward going and the inward turning. For they discovered, in the course of time, that they could not be 'clear' within the hedge if they restricted their range outside it; nor could they be effective outside until they pulled down the hedge itself.

They discovered, for example, that they had to go into Parliament. The anti-slavery campaign had been an entirely characteristic outcome of the Quaker conscience. Friends were clear about this, arriving at their judgement from their fundamental beliefs about the nature of man, being led, perceiving 'openings', moving from the inner to the outer. But the campaign involved them in some unquakerly activities. At the American end, the story of the underground railroad was one of high courage and selflessness, but also of some infringements of the Quaker standard of truth-telling: Friends learnt to lie in a good cause. The English campaign was one of politics and propaganda, and must have failed if Friends had not been allied with others with the same vision of man but without the same scrupulousness over membership of Parliament. The time came when the conscience had to adapt itself to the need for action. The first to enter, Joseph Pease (1799-1872), was the son of the Edward Pease who supported George Stephenson in his work on the steam engine, a Friend of the old school, who feared that the struggle against slavery was making Friends 'join too freely with persons who do not hold sound views regarding our Blessed Lord and the revelation of His will to man',[1] believing there were 'deadly snares' for 'members of our religious profession' in such unguarded activities. He wished his beloved Society to return to its past, and to 'plainness of speech and apparel'; and he was anxious about the creeping luxuriousness that permitted Friends to introduce 'pictures and fancy articles into the home', or enjoy 'a water goblet to each person'. His own conscience was severe with him:

> Condemned for time spent in looking over the *Illustrated London News*, and reading of its articles. This work is one of the attractive fascinations of the present time.[2]

He was dismayed when Joseph reported that he had been invited to stand for Parliament:

> Unless you are wholly regardless of all parental counsel, the advice of all your best friends, the domestic happiness of your family, your duties as a husband and a parent and a member of the Society of Friends, you could not for a moment entertain the idea of yielding under any contingency to become a representative of your countrymen in Parliament.[3]

Other Friends said much the same thing. But Joseph had

[1] *Diaries*, pp. 175, 176. [2] Ib., p. 297. [3] Ib., p. 65.

a conscience too, that led him on, and he entered Parliament in 1833, the first member in history to make an affirmation instead of taking an oath. He made no spectacular contribution during his nine years in the House, but he had opened the way to others: notably for John Bright (1811-1899), whose struggles for the repeal of the Corn Laws, for the extension of the franchise, and for the extension of liberties in India and Ireland were all genuinely Quaker outcomes within the world of compromise and the 'art of the possible', from which the pedantic Quaker conscience had for so long recoiled. Bright was able to stand firm, without compromise, on the Crimean War, when the historic testimony rang out: 'You must excuse me if I cannot go with you. I will have no part in this terrible crime.' In the abuse that followed, he showed too the old Quaker firmness under persecution; and the same directness of speech that gave Fox his power. For when, after the famous 'Angel of Death' speech, Disraeli approached him and said, 'Bright, I would give all I ever had to have made that speech you made just now,' Bright replied, 'Well, you might have made it if you had been honest.' The tension between conscience and action was still real, but it was held for Bright in a larger frame: 'conscience' was no longer a 'Quaker testimony' but the plain honesty of a man of good will and open eyes. It led him along with other honest men in the work of reform; it made him part company with them when the nation plunged into the folly of the Crimea.

Where Pease and Bright led, other Friends have followed. They were, as we should expect, among the last surviving Independent members; now they cheerfully accept the party whip, recognizing that even this is part of the machinery of government; and government they have always recognized, as part of the machinery of living.

Another area in which activity on the perimeter led to a

change at the centre was that of 'foreign missions'. Friends had suffered a curious disability here, arising from their reluctance to organize for action. 'Organization' meant 'creatureliness': in practical terms, it meant that some Friends would have to set up tasks to which they would engage others: and this was contrary to the spirit of 'leading'. Friends were meant to discover a concern in their own experience of their own situation, not to yield to the persuasion of others to fill a vacancy on a list. When, in 1830, a Quarterly Meeting suggested that Friends should 'take some more active measures for spreading the glad tidings of the gospel among the heathen', a Friend observed that 'many among us will be much astonished . . . I know not what we can understand by this, unless it may be that they wish to consider whether the time is not come for sending out ministers.'[1] It was to be some time before this blood-chilling possibility became fact, but in the meantime several Friends felt the need for action, and set out directly 'under concern'. There was Thomas Shillitoe (1754-1836), moving quietly through Europe, meeting little mystic groups like the early Seekers, working among the inmates of continental prisons, pressing his simple faith on kings and their families. There was Stephen Grellett (1773-1855),[2] with a route similar but more far-reaching, to Russia and the near East. There was Daniel Wheeler (1771-1840),[3] led on from a characteristically Quaker task of land-drainage in Russia to travels among convicts in Australia and finally a missionary effort in the South Seas.

All these journeys showed both the strength and weak-

[1] H. T. Hodgkin, *Friends Beyond Seas*, p. 28.

[2] From a French Catholic family, who had fought against the Revolution, and became a widely travelled evangelist and inspirer of Elizabeth Fry.

[3] Fought in the Napoleonic wars, turned Friend and farmer, acting as agricultural adviser to the Czar, Alexander I, and sailing the South Seas on missionary service for four years.

ness of the vestigial Quietist temper: they were personal, imaginative, wide-ranging; but they were unsystematic, unco-ordinated, unconsolidated. But in 1868 'The Friends' Foreign Missionary Association' was formed with the task of following up the concerns of individuals, and establishing the needs thus discovered as 'corporate concerns' of the Society as a whole. It was the first open recognition of the necessity for organization; and the work, and continuing, progressive work, was of itself a challenge to conscience. 'The world vision', said Henry T. Hodgkin of the eighteenth century, 'was replaced by the Inward Look.' Now it was to return.

But Friends were still in a dilemma. Quakerism originated as a commentary on the Christian tradition. 'You have learnt from without,' it said to Christians, 'now look within.' But what sort of a message was to be given to those who had not learnt at all?

The new missionary impulse arose from the evangelical mood that broke in on Friends from other churches, and assumed a confidence in bible teaching and preaching that early Friends would not have shared. For a time, therefore, there were tensions within the missionary effort, the desire to spread 'the glad tidings of the gospel among the heathen' in conflict with the desire to 'answer that of God in every man'. The latter impulse has never reached its own perfection, for its fulfilment demands a knowledge of the theology of other faiths which Friends have been averse from acquiring; but nevertheless it has nearly always been present in Quaker centres of effort, with the result that forms of worship and church organization have often been novel, with a sensitivity to indigenous habits some more confidently evangelical missions took longer to learn.

Despite this degree of dualism Quaker missions were able to develop certain recognizable and characteristic patterns.

They tended to begin in relief work, medicine, education, with the clearing away of obstacles to personal development which on any showing must be blinds against the Light. They became schools of living, structures for raising the standard and deepening the quality of life, and so releasing the hidden springs. They accepted, perforce, the 'outward', in the shape of a structure of leadership, instruction in basic Christian doctrine, and mechanism for church discipline; but the communities that grew around them soon developed something of their own way of life.

Meanwhile Friends had become aware that the home mission front was as much in need of attention as the foreign front. The Society took a census in 1850, and was shaken to discover that numerically it was in decline. One Friend, seeking an analysis of the situation, awarded a prize of a hundred guineas for the best essay on the causes of the decline. The winning essay, by John Stephenson Rowntree, boldly attacked the Quaker shibboleths: the peculiarity of the meeting for worship, which Friends had erected into a sacred form, without regard to the differing needs of the members; the weakness of ministry in the meetings, which he attributed to the assumption that ministry must be entirely unpremeditated, a direct word given by God for prophetic utterance; the isolation of Friends from the life and culture round them; their artificial peculiarities of dress and manner. On the decline in numbers he concludes that a third of the Friends who had married during the previous fifty years had been disowned for marrying non-Friends. 'Rich indeed must be that church which can spare such members for such a cause.'[1] The essay appeared at a time when Friends were disturbed, and ready for awkward truth, and when the young were already astir with the determination to turn testimony into mission.

[1] *Quakerism Past and Present*, p. 15.

Mission demands message: and under the pressures from new contacts Friends were driven to ask themselves what it was they had to say. A volume of essays by 'Three Friends', entitled *A Reasonable Faith*, appeared in 1884, challenging the evangelical assumption that the Bible was enough as a statement of faith for the contemporary world, and developing anew the early Quaker position on the inspiration of scripture: 'We,' they said, 'have access to the same spirit which inspired the sacred writers.' Revelation is progressive, and the Bible takes its due place in the story, but modern thought and the power of reason must play their part; and 'revelation' is not a static concept, turning only on a divine act from the beyond, but a dynamic one, taking account of variety and progress in man's insight and power to apprehend.

After a sharp explosion of dismay from the traditionalists, these views gathered support. A conference in Manchester in 1895 focused the new lines of thought on the relevance of the Quaker experience; and at a time when 'science' and 'religion' seemed locked in conflict Silvanus P. Thompson pressed the argument that the form of biblical myth may be rejected without loss to its meaning. The Bible, he reminded the conference, gave Fox practically his sole education, and he knew it and loved it as well as any man.

> Yet for all this he steadily refused, and his consistent followers have to this day refused, to call that precious book *The Word of God*. Now we can say to the scientific student . . . that we need not ask you to accept the Hebrew chronology or the Hebrew cosmology as a necessary part of an all-rounded and infallible Word of God . . . That which was spoken unscientifically in the childhood of the world by the unscientific Hebrew sage is no essential part of Christ's message to the world today.[1]

[1] Proceedings, Manchester Conference, pp. 362-8.

He pressed the attack home to the Quietist principle itself, and to the mental inertia that stemmed from it.

> We have no right to neglect our intellects any more than we have to neglect our bodies. Neither are we justified in refusing to think for fear that thought logically followed out might change opinions that we or our fathers have cherished . . . The faculty of reason, the noblest possession of a man's physical being, is a faculty not only to be prized, trained and used, but to be trusted and followed.

If Friends were to begin to think, they would need someone to help them to do it; and a plea began to be heard for the development of a teaching ministry, an active, effortful and creative ministry for which Friends would, quite deliberately, equip themselves. The concept of a professional body, trained and set aside, 'bred at Oxford or Cambridge', was still not to be considered, but a new Quaker habit established itself of attendance at summer schools and weekend settlements, in which not only were 'ministers' enabled to study and ponder, but less fluent Friends were aroused to a broader, more sophisticated view of their faith. These gatherings have become so familiar a part of the Quaker scene that even Friends with traces of the old Quietist temper would not regard them as 'organization' at all, though they are planned and arranged with care and foresight.

The Quaker method has here enriched, and been in turn enriched by, the practice of other churches. There is scholarship, discipline, control and direction; but there is also freedom-in-relation. The Quaker habits of open speech, readiness to listen to the unscholarly, assumption that agreement is to be found, concentration in the end on issues that arise in living and are not confined to the speculative—all this may be seen at work. The group encounter thus becomes a substitute for a trained priesthood; and at least lays the situation open for larger thought to set to work.

The last step in the modernization of the structure of the Society, in clearing and establishing the lines of communication in a group that was turning itself outwards, was the creation of an efficient committee structure. Other churches, with their well-established and easily adapted structures, would regard this process as merely the overdue importing of a little common sense. But to Friends it was a change not without pain, for specialist committees (for peace, for service overseas, for mission at home) smelled of professionalism, none the less sinister for being unpaid. But they had to come, for the role of the all-rounder in Christian living was destroyed along with the role of the all-rounder in life. A lay church, like society at large, had to channel its members' time and skill, and to focus its corporate action at particular points of decision. The harnessing of energies still relied on 'concern', and Friends were careful not to press each other into directions for which they felt no personal bent. But now there was machinery for continuing a concern beyond the lifetime, or the time of service, of the Friend who initiated it.

The underlying unity beneath all these shifts of emphasis is to be found in the rediscovery of the central meaning, though not yet the deep, explosive power, of early Quakerism. The leaders of thought often appealed, as we have seen Silvanus Thompson (1851-1912)[1] appeal to the witness of early Friends; and as those early Friends believed that Quakerism was 'primitive Christianity revived', so these later Friends sought to revive primitive Quakerism. This concept of revival was inevitably limiting, for the primitive can never be revived, but it served its turn, for it provided the motive to break the fossilized peculiarity of

[1] Elected to the Royal Society, 1891.

the Society; and it left Friends open to the language and thought-forms of the generation among whom they lived. They were ready now, not merely to offer service from an inherited and guarded strength, but to learn from others who were strong. They were once more able, as early Friends were so spontaneously and so effortlessly able, to speak and listen to other Christians. They were back in their true role, as partners in a dialogue between the traditional and the experimental.

X

The Quaker Role

THE DIALECTIC of Quaker history lies between dialogue and withdrawal. It began in dialogue, a painful dialogue in which a word to the many was sustained in the most painful of all forms of human confrontation, the acceptance of suffering. Then, partly because they had suffered enough, partly because others had learnt tolerance and to some extent indifference, Friends withdrew into the protection and refinement of their way of life. Now we see them emerging from their withdrawal, ready once more for dialogue.

They are themselves no longer peculiar. They wear the clothes of the day; they work alongside other people; they take responsibility, in politics, trade unions and industry, for actions that are less than perfect. They act and paint and make music. They can no longer be picked out of the crowd. At the same time, they find the Christian Church open to a renewal of the dialogue in a way that it has not been open for three hundred years. For the Christian Church is itself conducting the argument that originated in the seventeenth century about the relationship between inherited imagery and first-hand experience.

Rufus Jones, trying to identify the rudiments of the Quaker message, expresses himself, in 1927,[1] in language that curiously anticipates the theological debate of the

[1] *The Faith and Practice of the Quakers*, London, 1927, pp. 39ff.

nineteen sixties. Early Friends, he argues, did not succeed, as they claimed they were doing, in restoring to the world a replica of first-century Christianity.

> We shall not . . . find in the Quaker movement a replica of the first century. It is not that. If those early Quaker builders thought it was that, they were mistaken. What they did do, and do very well, was to lay hold upon certain basic principles and spiritual ideals which were admirably suited to the temper and trend of the modern world . . .
>
> What they did was to insist that religion is something that begins within the soul of man. They passed over, as Copernicus did, to a new centre . . . to ground religion for ever upon an inherent relation between God as living Spirit and the elemental spiritual nature of man. Religion, they believed, does not rise outside and flow in; it springs up inside and flows out.

Talk about God thus *begins*, though it will certainly not end, with talk about man's deepest personal experiences. And in this definition of religious discourse, all men are 'religious'. 'It is true, no doubt,' Rufus Jones continues,

> that many persons 'go through life' without being consciously aware of their high endowment, they accumulate 'things', live in their outside world, 'make good' . . . but . . . the *push for the beyond* is always there in us . . .

This is not yet the language of Tillich, but it is kindred imagery. And in elaborating on the 'push for the beyond', Rufus Jones comes very close to the current form of the argument about 'images':

> It is useless now to debate the question whether that divine trait belongs essentially to the human soul or is something supernaturally added to it as a free act of God . . . There is little doubt that many of the early Friends held the latter view, certainly Robert Barclay did. It was an age that did its thinking in pretty sharp dualisms. There had been then very little real adjustment to the revolutionary theory of Copernicus. There has been even yet very little attempt to think

> through what is involved in the new conception of the sky, which logically is more destructive of old theology than the theory of evolution is. In the seventeenth century, most people still thought of the sky as a crystalline dome, of heaven as 'up there', of God as dwelling yonder, of everything 'here below', including the human soul, as belonging to the 'natural sphere', and, consequently, as undivine and sundered from God.
>
> Whatever *partook of the divine,* and was to *operate spiritually,* must on this theory come from beyond the chasm which divided the two sundered spheres, and, therefore, be 'a supernatural agent'.

'We do not, most of us,' he concludes, 'think that way now.' And that, if we listen to Quaker discourse, we should agree to be true. The language in which Friends make their religious exchanges is realist language: it is not concerned with the supernatural, but with experiences, with 'happenings-in-here', events within the area of personal choice. There is no Quaker system of ideas, to be handed on from generation to generation in a package, to be accepted or reinterpreted by each generation: there is only a Quaker *method,* which begins 'inside'. The nearest Friends have ever come to a formulary is in their collection of *Advices and Queries,* which begin, not with God, but with 'looking' within. 'Take heed, dear Friends, of the promptings of love and truth in your hearts.' This, they say, is where it all begins.

If they were pressed on what they mean by 'love and truth', some Friends would still render their account in mystical, dualistic terms; but the majority would probably say something like this. 'When I use the word "promptings" I recognize that in most of the choices we make there is an element of doubt and conflict: that in the process of "making up my mind" I have to listen to voices from different "selves". Among these voices is one to which I wish particularly to listen; but my experience is that this voice is not as vociferous or compelling as many of the others. Greed, laziness, competitiveness, fear, lust—these are the things I am made of; and they rush up into my field of choice, or, more subtly, work beneath my consciousness, with pre-emptoriness and power. But if I wait long enough as I make my choice, I reach a deeper level of motive, in which I am aware of two quieter voices that seem on reflection to be more constructive, more insistent, than the others: the voices of "love" and "truth". By "love" I mean my sense of the importance of other people, the feeling that other people "matter" unconditionally, my sense that I ought to assert this importance. I mean also my awareness of their state of mind, the discovery I begin to make, when I *do* resolve to assert their importance, of their fears and hopes and needs, my "feeling sense of their condition". This "awareness of the other" remains relatively weak as a motive, partly because my instinctive make-up is always there first, partly because though I begin to learn more of the otherness of others, I am never near full understanding of their true need. But though "love" is weak, it can be discriminated and listened to: as the song of a bird in city traffic is weak, but can be picked out and listened to.

'By "truth" I mean a hunch I have that the choice I am making has somewhere within it the "right" answer, an answer somehow "built in" to the situation; that I need to find this answer; and that when it is found it will embrace both his condition and mine. It will be bigger than both of us, more "real" than the fears and hopes I am trying to rise above. I believe that if I can wait long enough, and reach deep enough, I shall arrive at a point where I say, "Yes, this is it". This point of insight seems somehow final, with its own "rightness", such as one experiences when a "sum" comes out.

'What I am saying to other Christians is that you all begin at the wrong point. You start with something "out there" —an abstract framework of belief, a ritual act, a picture of supernatural reality—while I start "in here" with an activity of my own vision and will, discriminating between experiences that thrust themselves upon my consciousness. You begin with image or notion : I begin with the working of conscience.'

The critic would at once fasten on the naivety of this statement, on the lavish, question-begging inverted commas, used as a recognition that there is a difficulty in the words and phrases, but at the same time a refusal to pursue the difficulty into any form of philosophical analysis. The Quaker is as tough-minded on this issue as the positivist philosopher, with the difference that the positivist says that because values cannot be discussed philosophically, they need not be discussed at all; while the Quaker says they must be discussed in commonsense terms. Problems of value-judgement will not be *cleared up* in such terms, but nor will they be cleared up in philosophical terms. They will not, indeed, be cleared up at all, in the sense that a structure can be erected, which will settle a man's problems for him. The making of value-judgements is an activity of the person involved in the situation; and though he may think as clearly as he can, the central issue is a personal one in which his imagination and emotion and will are all involved. He must, quite literally, *make* his choice. It is a situation that calls for creativeness, and not merely for a process of looking up the index for the 'answer'.

But this, the critic objects, is pure humanism. The distinctive note of Christianity is precisely this outward turning that you deny, this point of reference outside the personality which imports into his experience an imperative of belief and ethical choice: Christian worship is about Otherness, not inwardness. If you confine yourself to the exploration of the promptings of love and truth you do no more than the serious humanist who sets as the goal of human endeavour some such ideal as 'self-realization' or the 'fulfilment of human potentiality'. Even among humanists there are longer term goals than this: the notion of evolution carries something of an apocalyptic. Where is your apocalyptic? Where do you hope to arrive?

The Quaker answer to this is, Yes, of course. At this point we accept, without arguing, the kind of statement that you other Christians make about reality. We recognize, in these 'promptings', 'the leadings of the Holy Spirit of God . . . It is God's love that draws us to Him, a redemptive love shown forth in Jesus Christ in all His life and above all on the cross. He is the Way, the Truth, the Life.'[1] If you press us on what we mean by this kind of language, we can only say that we do not know. This is all imagery, which disappears into obscurantism when we try to analyse it, but which we use to convey our belief that there is something more in all this than a kind of aesthetic experience. These 'promptings' come from somewhere, we say. They are not just ourselves in a peculiarly sensitive mood. They come upon us. They are imperative. And it is this belief that separates us from the atheist, who would deny that they correspond to anything that could meaningfully be called reality at all.

'We use your language,' Friends would go on, 'though we cannot analyse it, to carry the kind of meaning John Robinson was dealing with when he wrote, "Is there any sense in which one can meaningfully talk of anything unconditional or absolute? The true . . . atheist would

[1] General Advices, see *Church Government*, pub. Central Offices of the Society of Friends.

answer No. And this is the real dividing line between those who can speak of God and those who cannot."[1] We use this language because only so can we convey our sense that the "promptings" are unconditional. We refuse to analyse this language because such an analysis is "notional"; and because the "promptings", though unconditional in the situation in which they arise, are specific to the situation. They concern the moment, in which two or more individuals are involved in a situation and a relationship that have never occurred before and will never occur again. Or they concern one man alone, facing "God" in depths of his own being that lie far beneath the crude work of words. In all this, all we can be conscious of is "the Word for the Now". We use language that implies the existence of a "speaker" because "words" are "spoken". But we will not go on to tell you about the "speaker" : we can only talk about our hearing of the speech.'

The 'hearing of the speech' comes in two forms: in the withdrawal of worship, and in the engagement of life in which conscience is awakened. Friends have never sought to distinguish between these two. They know they are 'different', but they would regard any attempt to lay down priorities of relative importance as meaningless, just as it would be to attempt to distinguish the roles of the left and right leg in walking. In worship, there is discoverable a level of personal insight in which the 'promptings' may be perceived. In action, the 'promptings' must be obeyed, however loud the counter-voices of selfish impulse. Worship may bring the worshipper to a point of vantage from which his whole life of action is seen in a new perspective. Faithfulness in action brings the actor to a level from which his worship can reach deeper yet. It is all one. But in both

[1] The reply to Alasdair MacIntyre's charge that John Robinson is an atheist, in *Encounter*, September and October, 1963.

worship and action, over-much attention to the outward may prevent the reaching of the true level.

Caroline Stephen describes her first meeting for worship as precisely this 'finding of a place' where reality might be known. She was invited to a Quaker meeting at

> a moment of need, for I was beginning to feel with dismay that I might not much longer be able conscientiously to continue to join in the Church of England service; not for want of appreciation of its unrivalled richness and beauty, but from doubts of the truth of its doctrines, combined with a growing recognition that to me it was as the armour of Saul in its elaboration, and in the sustained pitch of religious fervour for which it was meant to provide an utterance . . . On one never-to-be-forgotten Sunday morning, I found myself one of a small company of silent worshippers, who were content to sit down together without words, that each one might feel after and draw near to the Divine Presence, unhindered at least, if not helped, by any human utterance . . . My whole soul was filled with the unutterable peace of the undisturbed opportunity for communion with God, with the sense that at last I had found a place where I might, without the faintest suspicion of insincerity, join with others in simply seeking His presence. To sit down in silence could at least pledge me to nothing; it might open to me (as it did that morning) the very gate of heaven.[1]

Despite the supernaturalist imagery here, the basic contention is 'experimental': that to wait in company in the silence, committed only to commitment, is both relaxing and tautening. It 'lets a man be' and brings him into 'being'. This is, in the end, all that happens in a meeting for worship. Friends may offer words, terse, unemotional, impersonal in tone; but the words are not worship, though they may promote it. The worship is the shared privacy on the personal frontier. And in the worship there is a kind of movement, some 're-structuring' of experience, some fusing

[1] *Quaker Strongholds*, London, 1890, pp. 12, 13.

of dissonant elements in the personality, some release of energy, that comes as illumination, either of a particular situation, or of some permanent dimension of the human situation.

Our persistent critic would fasten on two elements in this account: the reference to the Church of England service, and the sitting down in silence that 'could at least pledge me to nothing'. Caroline Stephen, he would observe, was an Anglican who found the demands of her familiar religious imagery too much for her, and found release, escape, peace of mind, in the undemanding Quaker silence. Early Friends, he would continue, were members of other churches, who had, in precisely the same way, found their framework too demanding, and had found escape and peace in silent communion. But this is not to *begin* with the immediate and first-hand: it is to turn to it in the light of much learning from the tradition, at second hand. This is nothing more than an unusually rapid movement from the traditional to the experimental. It is not in any way a new departure. It does not start, with the mind and soul a *tabula rasa*, in a raw encounter with the unknown God.

Then, he would continue, what of this 'pledge to nothing'? Where do you go from here? Do you remain, 'committed to commitment', but never arriving at a general view that you can share with others? Is your experience, not only in its beginning but in its end, private and incommunicable? Is this vision of the 'very gate of heaven' simply a moment of private ecstasy, or can we talk about it?

The Quaker would agree that the meaning of his experience is difficult to 'talk about'. This is at the heart of his case: the case against 'notions', the case for silence. But he would deny that this makes it a 'moment of private ecstasy', with no meaning beyond itself, and no possibility of sharing. It is *penetrable*: it may be gone through; and on the other side is the recognition of Christ, standing as 'other', over against the private whim; and recognizable, about whom men can agree in the recognition. This, they would say, is the meaning of Fox's experience; and it remains accessible. The road is from conscience to Christ.

> How are we to be saved? How are we to realize the Christ of our Gospel? . . . Beyond all question a first consideration is sincerity . . . We must honestly seek the true life, we must honestly wish to escape the toils of self-love . . . but . . . I must seek not merely to lop off but to grow . . . And here is a difficulty. In practical experience how am I to know what is meant by listening to the voice of Christ, obeying Him and following Him? . . . Conscience is a guide I can follow. For example, be thoughtful of others, even in little things. Make a practice of forgetting yourself. In the past it was always *I*, what do they say and think of *me*, am *I* getting the recognition that is my due? . . . But I cannot rest satisfied here. I seek not only discipline but victory. I want to know not only conscience but Christ. Yes, but to the sincere experimentalist, using his conscience as a guide, and seeking always to focus his life on that of Jesus Christ, as he knows Him in the Gospels, and recognizes Him in His faithful disciples, there comes a time when the line between conscience and Christ grows very thin. There comes a time when the higher life of which I am always aware, and which I have tried to follow, becomes so merged in my thought of Christ and my devotion to Him, that I can hardly distinguish the two in my mind.[1]

'Knows Him in the Gospels,' 'recognizes Him in His faithful disciples'—and then 'the line between conscience and Christ grows very thin': here is the work of love and truth seen in history and in other men, and the inner vision being refined to the point of meeting. This is the argument of one who, trying to teach sensitivity to colour, says, 'You

[1] John Wilhelm Rowntree, *Essays and Addresses*, London, 1906, pp. 399-401.

must start by looking at colours. Anything you hear about colour will be "notional", abstract, for blueness or redness cannot be described. So you must look at your blues and reds; *and* at other men's blues and reds; *and* at *this* blue and red, which are the richest we know. Then the day will come when you can discriminate with confidence among the mixed shades in which you work. Your own sense of blueness will merge indistinguishably with the model.'

The 'model' is not to be met in abstractions or descriptions, but only in seeing; because the model is personal. And only those who have learnt to see, on the personal level, will see him. But he is, says the experimentalist, nevertheless 'there' to be seen. He 'is'. And though the worshippers may not agree on what they see in Christ—as we do not agree with each other on what we see in any person—they can agree in the seeing.

At this point, most Christians would object, the argument stops short and becomes inadequate. For its completion it must go on to answer the question, But what is it you see?

A merely descriptive account of experience is not enough to make it useful to others. The 'experimentalist', whether in science or religion, cannot simply describe 'what happens': he must proceed to some explanation of what happens, to some generalization from his experience. And here, in seeking to use the image of the encounter with Christ as his account of the ultimate, authoritative and unifying experience, he must begin some kind of analysis of the 'meaning' of the image. As Gregor Smith puts it:

> If I ask the most urgent and personal question of all, 'What must I do to be saved?' I intend no blasphemy or ultimate scepticism when I say that the answer . . . 'Believe on the Lord Jesus Christ', does not answer my question, today, in my circumstances . . . directly or satisfactorily. It leaves me, and my companions in this modern world,

> both those within and those without the Church, with many questions, the question about the nature of belief, the question about who Jesus is, and where, and how, and the question about the substance of salvation itself. In other words a great deal of re-thinking requires to be done which will be neither biblical theology by itself nor systematic theology by itself, but an existential assessment of the Bible and the world which will uncover the almost entirely dissipated claim of real transcendence as an existent force *within* this world.[1]

Friends would certainly claim Gregor Smith as an ally, and would endorse his judgement on orthodox theology, and the need for an 'existential assessment' to 'uncover the . . . claim of real transcendence'. But they would not, themselves, have written the first words, raising those questions about Jesus. They would not welcome a call to proceed from the experimental to the theoretical; for they conceive themselves to be 'against theory'.

Yet on the analogy with science which early Friends used to illustrate their new point of departure, the experimental is a means to the theoretical: the concrete instance is an object for generalization. The difference between scientific theory and religious dogma is not that one is 'real' and the other 'abstract': it is that theory is erected inductively from the facts as observed, while the dogma is arrived at deductively from revelation, or from some overriding principle. The Quaker argument that religious thinking begins in the experimental would be acceptable to many more traditional Christians provided it led on to some recognizable generalizations and produced a 'theory'.

In practice, much description of the Quaker experience stops short at mere description. Consider the following.

[1] Ronald Gregor Smith: *The New Man: Christianity and Man's Coming of Age*, London, 1956, pp. 95-6.

The thing is just to live the highest life we know and leave everything else.[1]

To you who are seekers, to you, young and old who have toiled all night and caught nothing, but who want to launch out into the deeps and let down your nets for a draught, I want to speak as simply, as tenderly, as clearly as I can. For God *can* be found. There *is* a last rock for your souls, a resting-place of absolute peace and joy and power and radiance and security. There is a Divine Center into which your life can slip, a new and absolute orientation in God, a Center where you live with Him and out of which you see all of life, through new and radiant vision, tinged with new sorrows and pains, new joys unspeakable and full of glory . . . One knows at first hand what the old inquiry meant, 'Has Truth been advancing among you?'[2]

And finally, from Corder Catchpool, a statement of great beauty and power to move, yet disconcerting in its implication that 'theory' comes to an end when 'experience' is once attained:

What then really is Christianity, if much that takes its name so fails to satisfy? I must face that problem; I felt no confidence that I was equal to it. But I seemed to be at least 50 per cent rationalist in make-up; that part of me demanded an answer. I began, fumblingly, an attempt to reason it out. I was by now high up on the moraine. The lazy clouds, that had hung all day as a light veiling about the snow-powdered rock peaks, were just breaking up on the clear splendour of sunset. The dazzling mantles of Combin and Courbassière caught the last rays. It was no moment for reasoning. Too often my spiritual life runs shamefully shallow, lamentably in need of more living water from the eternal springs. May I be pardoned—I was utterly unworthy—but at that moment there swept over me unbidden, the *experience* of Christ. No more tiresome ratiocination, interpretations or misinterpretations, dogmas and differences. Just the fact that, in Christ, God was and is sharing the tragedy and sorrow, and the joy

[1] George Lloyd Hodgkin, in L. Violet Hodgkin: *George Lloyd Hodgkin* (a memoir), 1921, p. 119.

[2] Thomas R. Kelly, *A Testament of Devotion*, 1941, pp. 18-19.

> of the world. And—most glorious assurance—in his death and resurrection he faced the worst the world can do, faced these same problems and perplexities with all their mental anguish, which so often beat us till we cry inwardly for quarter—Christ faced them and triumphed over them and through them, with and for man in his struggle after righteousness, for all time.[1]

'No more tiresome ratiocination,' says Corder Catchpool. But then, it must be asked, how can you say what you mean?

It would be open to Friends to take up a more radical position: to aver that no theory is possible, to make no use of Christian imagery, to insist that reason does not come into the business at all. Whether or not they would be 'Christian' in such a case is perhaps doubtful. What it is not open for them to do is to declare that religion begins in experience and has nothing to do with abstract inheritance, and then make use of Christian imagery to say, You see we get there in the end. The meaning of the encounter in the silence slips through the mesh unless some kind of analysis —theoretical, hypothetical—is offered.

The necessity for this has not gone entirely unperceived. At the Friends World Conference in 1952 a group of Friends advanced the case for a Quaker theology. Frozen formularies, they agreed, were to be avoided, but

> verbal statements are a valuable means of clarifying thought. If kept subject to constant revision, they may help us in reaching unity. They are also helpful in conveying our faith to others . . . Thought and commitment mutually interact . . . If theology is defined as 'thinking about God', it is a proper activity for Quakers.[2]

And, more pungently, John Harvey warns the Society

[1] From William R. Hughes, *Indomitable Friend*, 1956, p. 205.
[2] Friends World Conference, Oxford, 1952. Report: *What is our faith?*

that the testimony against theology is nowadays a tilting against dream windmills:

> It ought to be recognized that at the present time, at least in this country, the real danger is not from a too narrow, cramping and militantly dogmatic theology, but rather from an inveterate haziness of mind, a half-heartedness and general belittlement of the importance of true thinking in religion. And the final outcome of this is the assumption . . . that Christianity may indeed reasonably claim to be 'good', that is to put forward an elevated ethical standard and an edifying moral idealism, but makes and can make no claim to be 'true'. I do not think it likely that terms like 'theology', 'dogma', and 'creed' will ever evoke enthusiasm among members of the Society of Friends. But it ought to be possible to allay what almost amounts to a phobia with regard to them.[1]

The 'phobia', as we have seen, is in some measure a vestigial attitude from the early days, a transfer from the days when there was too much thinking and arguing about the wrong issues to a day when there is virtually no thought or argument about any issues. Another reason for the naivety of the Society lies in its lay structure: a group in which nobody is trained for the priesthood will tend to take a 'commonsense' view of its fundamental ideas.

Be that as it may, the Society is becoming aware that its true testimony here is not the denial of theology so much as the assertion that each generation must make its theology anew; that there is a progress from the inherited tradition to the immediate experience, and thereafter a process of reconstruction, of demythologizing and re-mythologizing, of theory-building, in which the new generalizations are made from the new experience. But this new theory-making Friends have not begun to do. They welcome it in other churches, but have not significantly engaged in it

[1] *The Salt and the Leaven* (Swarthmore Lecture), 1947, p. 76. This argument is not often heard among Friends. But John Harvey was Professor of Philosophy, University of Leeds.

themselves. And it may be that their inheritance and lay-structure operate so strongly against it that they never will.

Those Friends who view this prospect with equanimity would describe the role of the Society as being not so much theory-building as decision-making. The weakness in theory, they say, is a strength in practical affairs. The layman is continually involved in the pragmatic and particular; and his test of 'rightness' is not coherence with a general theory but success in practice. He asks not so much, Is this 'true'? as Does this work out well? Ultimately, he would agree, the 'true' and the 'right' must cohere, but in the business of living the layman asks for a more readily available test of 'rightness' than coherence within a set of abstract principles.

The Quaker 'test of rightness' is unanimity within the face-to-face group, achieved after sufficient deliberation to ensure that the question has been taken to the depths of personal concern appropriate to it. The Quaker contribution to Christian decision-making is thus an account of method rather than an assertion of principle. The 'method' is now tolerably familiar. A small group of Friends meets to do business, and begins with a time of worship, long enough to 'centre down' to a level where the accidental—prejudice, whim, fear, selfish interest—begins to edge away from the centre of attention. The agenda is then considered, in much the same way as any committee considers its agenda, but the conditions are different from most committees. There is no chairman, armed with authority: only a 'clerk' at the table charged with the duty of catching eyes, both of those who speak and of those who only think and nod, and of drafting and re-drafting a minute that represents the 'sense of the meeting', a minute that is read aloud and pulled about until it is 'right'. No votes are taken, and the question is never 'put'. It is considered to be settled only when all present are convinced that the 'right' decision has been reached, when they have 'recognized the depth', in much the same way as they recognize the depth in a meeting for worship.

No method practised by human beings is safe against error, and even in their unanimity Friends are often mistaken in their decisions. But three centuries of experience of the method leave Friends convinced that certain elements in it tend towards right decisions. First, the group itself must be a genuine, face-to-face group. It must be small enough for the members to see and hear each other; and it will be the more effective and dynamic as the members know each other in their ordinary lives and become aware of each other's strengths and weaknesses. The optimum size of such a group will vary with the matter in hand. Ten or a dozen can do work of a complexity beyond the reach of thirty. Thirty or forty can deepen and sustain a concern more creatively than a group of ten. Anything beyond this thirty or forty tends to become merely a means of informing or controlling, of spreading the area of application rather than of genuine decision-making.

The second essential condition is that nobody should claim, by reason of his status or even of his expert knowledge, any special power of decision. Expert knowledge will be present, and will be needed: but it must be made available to the group. The expert must explain himself: and this explanation is salutary for the expert, as well as helpful to the group. The Friend who customarily delivers himself of good sense (the 'weighty Friend' as he is wryly called) establishes for himself a habit of being listened to, but he is not trusted for this 'weight'. The weighty Friend who speaks, for the nonce, without due thought, is soon made to think again.

The third condition is the understanding that the reaching of unity takes precedence over the need for coming to a decision. At first sight, this seems the wrong priority: surely the decision is more important than cosy feelings of amity? But no, the Friend would reply. We are here dealing with the principle of authority. Without a dogma or a rule book, we must accept something that overrides the play of whimsy; and what we have accepted is unity in the vision of rightness. Until all present have seen it, we cannot be satisfied that it has been seen at all. When a scientist wants to make a point, he makes it to fellow scientists; and he has not made it until they have agreed with him. Similarly, a Friend has not made his point until it has been 'seen' by at least all present. This is why voting is irrelevant; and why, too, speed may be dangerous. A decision made when only two-thirds are convinced will be the wrong one, either 'wrong' because it is, simply, mistaken, or—and this certainly—wrong because it will fail to call out the depths of active dedication needed for its fulfilment; or—and this most certain of all—wrong because a series of such decisions will destroy the trust and love from which further insight springs. It is better for the group to postpone a decision, and seem to be ineffective, than to seal off the members from each other. Even the 'right' decision becomes the 'wrong' one if it is reached in such a way as to foul the springs of love. If you believe that the characteristic mark of Christian decisions is that they are 'decisions for others', then 'the others', the principle of otherness, must be fully, weightily present through the whole process. And if, furthermore, they are *decisions*, then every person present must feel both the challenge and opportunity to decide.

When these three conditions are satisfied, there is still no 'guarantee' of right decision or further progress. But there is the assurance that the conditions of progress will be preserved. There will be meetings that fail; but when they have failed they still leave the channels open to life.

There are, however, certain limitations inherent in the system, even at its best. The Society of Friends has much experience of small-group work, little of the manipulation of a large community. Where a single meeting grows too large, or too fluid in membership, to permit of genuine face-to-face relationships, it loses its characteristic quality: and decision-making becomes a routine affair, falling into the hands of a few members. Further, the necessity for the 'expert' to lay aside his special status may—where the task calls for daily, tactical decision, as in the management of an institution, muddle and hamstring the whole process. A committee may have a series of 'stops in the mind' simply because the minds are incapable of moving. And the history of Quaker institutions has a curiously high proportion of conflicts arising from amateur incompetence. Finally, the overriding necessity of unity may delay a decision to the point where a decision has been made by default. To postpone saying Yes too long is, after all, to say No.

These 'negatives' of the Quaker method are important, because here is, undoubtedly, one of the gifts that Quaker experience offers to a Church drawing towards unity, and at the same time facing the problem of the layman's role. The operation of a small-group method of Christian action is of unique value; but it cannot be transferred *tout pur* to the large-group situation. It may well be one of the reasons why the Society of Friends itself stays so small, that the life goes out of it when the numbers pass a certain critical point. And it can certainly be no part of the Quaker case that this is the only possible form of decision-making. The lesson here for Friends is one that they have, indeed, begun to learn: that different tasks require different structures; and that specialist committees and the hierarchies of institutions need a degree of trust and autonomy that may, on the surface, conflict with their basic principles. The lesson for other Christians, who have articulated their structures of leadership, is that innovation from 'below' is not as dangerous as is sometimes thought; and that speed of decision may sometimes be purchased at too great a price.

A classic instance of the difficulty of large-group relationships has been offered recently by the pamphlet, *Towards a Quaker View of Sex,*[1] which represented an attempt by a group of concerned Friends to persuade the Society along the lines of the 'new morality'. The normal method of effecting changes in the attitude of the Society is the promotion of an individual 'concern', aired in a member's own meeting, and, if his fellow-members are 'in unity' with it, pressed on through Monthly Meeting and perhaps Quarterly Meeting to Yearly Meeting. This pamphlet arose in another way, when a number of Friends were drawn together by a common experience of the problem presented by homosexuality, in the concrete form of 'young Quaker students, faced with homosexual difficulties, who came to older Friends for help and guidance'. The group felt that 'the Society of Friends as such had little to say to people troubled sexually, and that at the same time many Friends were in serious doubt whether the Church's traditional view spoke to this condition'. And so they settled down together to discover what the Society of Friends 'as such' had to say to this condition.

Here is a situation which the Society is not sufficiently accustomed to deal with. The members of the group came from different parts of the country: they were 'specialists',

[1] Published for the group by the Friends Home Service Committee, 1963.

in the sense that they were all involved, as teachers, counsellors or psychiatrists, in the situation. In consequence, they had no obvious channel of communication, 'up' through the Society. They therefore wrote a pamphlet, which they unwisely released, with full publicity, to an eager press, before the Society had had time to subject the group to any form of Quaker discipline.

It was not long before the group discipline began to work, in the form of letters to *The Friend*, attacking both the matter of the argument and the manner of its presentation; and in due course pressure exerted through Meeting for Sufferings for a revision of the pamphlet and for safeguards against similar episodes in the future.

The demand for revision was in line with characteristic Quaker practice. The classic formula, 'individual concern → correction by group → group-concern' has here been transposed into large-group terms: the small group publishes its statement, the large-group gets to work on it, and there emerges (it is hoped, and in due time) a statement that broadly represents the common view. When, in this instance, the small group were criticized for their use of 'Quaker' in the title, which seemed to implicate all Friends, the authors replied, perfectly correctly, that they also used the word 'towards', and thus made plain that they were engaged in attitude-forming and not in moral dogmatizing. They were not 'stating Quaker principle', which, on principle, cannot be stated, but 'arousing Quaker concern'.

The argument begins, also, in classic Quaker style, with the reality of the human situation, and with the anxious guilt that arises when 'experience' (whether insight into fact or impulse to act) no longer corresponds with codes derived from the experience of the past. The fact is, it is urged, that the sexual code is no longer observed. We are faced today by new developments:

A. A great increase in adolescent sexual intimacy.

B. An increase in transient pre-marital sexual intimacies generally. It is fairly common in both young men and women with high standards of general conduct and integrity to have one or two love affairs, involving intercourse, before they find the person they will ultimately marry.

C. It is even more common for those who intend to marry to have intercourse before the ceremony. This is true, probably, of the majority of young people in all classes of society, including those who often have a deep sense of responsibility.

D. The incidence of extra-marital intercourse is great, but it is not possible to estimate whether there is an increase. There must be very many instances which do not lead to divorce or obvious harm and which are kept secret.

In their consideration of this the members of the group encountered 'tragic case-histories, outrageous miscarriages of justice'; and from their deeply felt concern they turned to the question, 'Has the Society of Friends any characteristic word to say?' They quote, as their point of departure, a recognition, already approved by Yearly Meeting, of the variety that in fact occurs in the experience of marriage:

> For some, there is a monogamy so entire that no other love ever touches it; but others 'fall in love' time and time again, and must learn to make riches of their affection without destroying their marriage or their friends. Let us thank God for what we share, which enables us to understand; and for the infinite variety in which each marriage stands alone.[1]

Then comes the question: How must we now define a moral code? Where, in all this, come statements about 'right' and 'wrong'?

[1] *Christian faith and practice in the experience of the Society of Friends*, 1960, §493.

From this point the pamphlet demonstrates both the strength and weakness of the Quaker habit of mind. The strength—the strength that has always been there—lies in the passionate integrity with which personal needs are understood and affirmed. Man is lord even of the Sabbath, lord even of theological propositions, and lord even of sexual convention. The homosexual is not outcaste, for his actions spring from a nature he did not choose, and within his actions there is the possibility of—indeed the challenge to—a 'kind of loving':

> It is the nature and quality of the relationship that matters: one must not judge it by its outward appearance but by its inner worth. Homosexual affection can be as selfless as heterosexual affection, and therefore we cannot see that it is in some way morally worse.

The same approach is made to extra-marital relations:

> our approach has to be through compassion—the reverse of moral judgement.

And the argument concludes in persuasion towards education 'for sincerity', for John Macmurray's definition of chastity as 'sincerity in the expression of what we feel . . . the fundamental virtue, from one point of view, of a Christian morality . . . the condition of personal integrity.'[1]

This argument is a micro-cell of the total Quaker argument: that general propositions do not 'speak to the condition' of the individual; that life cannot be contained by prescriptions from the past; that where life asserts itself stern moral judgements are beside the point; that persons who 'wander' (and do we not all 'wander' in some of our thought and action?) are still persons, still capable of per-

[1] In the essay, 'The Virtue of Chastity' in *Reason and Emotion*, 1935.

sonal responses and growth; and that such persons are helped by the affirmation of their personal worth and hindered by its denial. This, says the Quaker group, is basic Christianity. Christianity is concerned primarily with the personal; and within the personal with the growing point for the future. To use language that Friends would prefer to eschew, it is concerned with the forgiveness and redemption of the sinful children of God. In consequence, there are no Christian moral judgements, if those words are taken to mean systems for the assessment and allocation of guilt. The Christian experience takes us beyond the law.

The pamphlet fulfils its claim to be a contribution 'towards a Quaker view of sex' in facing, more specifically than Christians usually care to do, the implications of this principle. 'Society', and particularly Christian society, is too easily shocked by what should not be shocking, and extends condemnation to persons whose only 'fault' is to be imprisoned in circumstance, or to respond to life instead of to institutions.

This is the Quaker strength, this insistent personal reference. The Quaker weakness lies in the neglect of the general principle, the inherited attitudes, the custom and code within which the person grows, and without which 'the personal' is unattainable. Children grow up by learning the 'rules of the game'. They mature beyond childhood by seeing what the rules are for, and then playing the game with insight and individuality. But until the rules are clear, the 'game' is not in being. Moral judgements are the rules of the game; and while they are virtually useless as a means of judging the value of the play, they are necessary as a means of learning how to play. There needs to be some kind of codified experience, some general understanding of how things 'go', before the individual can bring his insight to bear on the situation. There needs, in a word, to be theory. The traditional theory may be dismissed as no longer applicable, but some sort of theory must take its place. And at this point of theory-making, the pamphlet becomes inadequate. The questions are raised, 'When is it right to have sexual intercourse, if it is not to be confined wholly to marriage? . . . Can we not say that God can enter any relationship in which there is a measure of selfless love?' Then the argument proceeds:

> There are no clear-cut answers . . . precisely because we are dealing with human relationships at their deepest, the point where rules are irrelevant. But the point where rules cease to apply is also the point at which our first and greatest need is to seek the will of God . . . If the traditional code seems now to be of little value, either in restraining us or in pointing out the way to generous living, then more than ever we need the presence of God in our judgements and decisions. And Christianity, precisely because it is concerned with the quality of human relationships, is more relevant to the unforeseen and the intensely difficult than it is to the neatly patterned way of life.

As a statement of what happens at 'the point where rules are irrelevant' this may be beyond criticism, as it is beyond analysis. But a theory must include some description of procedure *before* the moment arrives. How does a man learn to behave? The Quaker prescription is the face-to-face encounter. But moral problems are not to be solved entirely in face-to-face terms: they require also some understanding and acceptance of corporate intention. Moral education begins in the scrutiny of institutions, however far it must later progress to the imaginative entry into the personal situation. The Quaker argument, beginning at the point where the rules have become irrelevant, remains a commentary on the rules: it never succeeds in becoming a substantial theory.

The same is true of the well-established Quaker habit of

conscientious objection to military service. It originated, as we have seen, in George Fox's refusal of arms on the ground of his Christian vocation, his entry on 'that life and power that took away the occasion of all wars'. War, he was saying, was an anti-Christian way of dealing with conflicts between peoples. He then justified his personal refusal on grounds that he, he himself, was called on to live according to the full command of the Kingdom: 'I told them I was come into the covenant of peace which was before wars and strifes were.'

Today the peace testimony would be defended on the same grounds: that it is unchristian to fight, that 'Christian work' cannot be done that way; and that Christians are called to do, at whatever cost, the Christian work:

> The Quaker testimony . . . is based ultimately on the conception of that of God in every man to which the Christian in the presence of evil is called on to make appeal, following out a line of thought and conduct which, involving suffering as it may do, is, in the long run, the most likely to reach to the inward witness and so change the evil mind into the right mind. This result is not achieved by war.[1]

The characteristic Quaker logic is at work here: from an insight into a quality of life to a personal expression of it. The generalization and the interpretation are both impregnable: the generalization that, in the end, this is the way to live, and the personal interpretation for those who are aware of the vocation. But there is another question to be asked, which the Quaker testimony has never answered: What of those who have not arrived at this point of insight? Does the 'law' still hold for those not yet ready for the 'glorious liberty of the sons of Christ'? In practical terms, ought governments to keep order? The form in

[1] A. Neave Brayshaw, *The Quakers, their story and message*, 1921, p. 45.

which the problem posed itself in earlier times was the status of the magistrate, and this Friends were able to accept. Today it emerges in a more difficult form: Would you be ready to fight in a United Nations force, dedicated to the maintaining of law when 'glorious liberty' is impossible and inglorious anarchy imminent? This issue the Society of Friends has not yet faced; and it may well be that the next Friendly rumpus will be about a pamphlet 'Towards a neo-Quaker view of war'. In the meantime, most Quakers remain with a clear sense of individual vocation, but no general, applicable statement on the political realities of a world not yet in the 'life and power' that takes away 'the occasion of all wars'.

In all this, theology, worship, moral and political life, the Quaker message remains clear and challenging: Your traditions are not enough; your notions must come alive in experience, your moral rules must be dissolved in love, your hymns of praise must be sung in the silence of the heart. But the catholic Christian question remains, equally clear and challenging: True, they are not enough, but can you do without them? Do you want to destroy the law? Or will you keep faith with us, in our hope to fulfil it?

XI

Quakerism and the Church

THE BASIC questions with which this study began were the questions posed to all Christian sects by the mere existence of the ecumenical movement: Why do you stand alone? What is it your concern to defend? Is it something that a united church must inevitably lose? And if so, is the 'something' of such deep importance that, to preserve it, you must continue in your isolation? What, at bottom, is your effort about?

As we have considered the Quaker story through its three hundred years it has become clear that it is not, as the first Friends thought, about a complete substitute for the traditional Christian Church. It is rather about the tradition, about the way the tradition should be held and interpreted. It is a warning against traditionalism, an assertion of the evolutionary element within the tradition, a reminder of the novelty of the life of each new generation, shaped and brought to maturity within the tradition but incessantly challenged to explore beyond it.

Quakerism is the antithesis to the thesis of the Christian tradition, an element in the total Christian dialectic, a 'side' in the Christian conversation, a theme in the Christian symphony. Other Christians, from time to time, state the Quaker theme, but no other Christians have disposed their worship and church order around this theme alone. There is here, therefore, a unique Quaker role, a special message from Quakers to the Church, which it is laid on them to sustain until the time comes when the Christian symphony sounds in its fullness from the whole orchestra.

In the meantime there seem to be two special points of contact at which Friends offer their conversation. The first is a word of comfort and invitation to those who find themselves at odds with Christian 'machinery', whether credal, ritual, or administrative; those who have 'doubts', and find a particular dogma difficult to swallow. They cannot make sense of the doctrine of the Trinity, or the Virgin Birth; or they are out of tune with a form of worship, or they find the vicar pompous and overbearing. They are conscious of a dualism in their lives, in which they are made to oscillate between two ways of interpreting experience, two frames of reference that do not seem to meet: the one revelationary, supernatural, claiming an authority that fails to justify itself, terribly certain about reality 'out there'; the other exploratory, natural, claiming no authority save the two basic facts of the human existence: 'I' and 'others', and so reaching out towards the misty frontiers with no certainty, but only commitment to the teaching. To such people Friends say, quite simply, You can come out of all this, and sit down in silent communion, and find your belief and make your offering where you are. You will be surrounded by others doing the same thing; and you will help each other along.

Much effort has recently been put into an advertising campaign (about which many old-style Friends have suffered many 'stops in the mind') through newspaper and poster, the object of which is to inform and invite rather than persuade or proselytize.

> QUAKERS BELIEVE that in silence God speaks to each one of us, and that we are able to hear. Therefore Quakers meet in silence as the basis of their worship.

> QUAKERS BELIEVE that Christianity is a practical religion, to be lived out in daily life.
>
> Christ's light shows us the way;
> Christ's love gives us the strength;
> Christ's example gives us courage.
>
> Membership is open to those who share our outlook, and who, in worshipping with us, find themselves 'at home'. That simple expression is not out of place, for the Quaker way of life leads us to think of men and women the world over as parts of the family of God.

This last expresses fairly enough the spirit of Quaker evangelism, gentle in tone, directed to those who 'need' the Friendly community. Those who respond are met by a batch of literature, by conversation and perhaps by an invitation to a weekend conference—these last rediscovering the early Quaker experience that 'seeking' is more exciting than having given up looking. In this process of experimental encounter, Friends often find that some of these enquirers want something Friends cannot give. The task is then to direct them towards another destination—a task performed on a set of hunches about the temperamental typology of the churches, a vague sense that different structures of community meet different personal needs, and make different demands on personal gifts. Friends would not wish to analyse these hunches, or to be explicit about the psychological features of the Quaker type, or even to admit that there is such a type. But though these hunches can never be verified, they reflect a reality in the ecumenical situation. The sects are concerned with different emphases rather than with different 'truths'; and as the denominations look outwards on the total Christian task they become aware that it demands all the variety and richness of the total Christian experience.

The second Quaker word is one addressed to members of

all the churches, particularly, perhaps, those who are too little out of tune with their tradition, and have no doubts at all. To these Friends say, We do not want you to become Friends, and we are not 'preaching' to you. But we do ask you to consider your inheritance and ask what it means now, in the present moment, in your own personal lives. Consider your creeds, your great statements of what you believe, designed to safeguard the 'truth' from ignorance and prejudice and private whimsy. Consider the danger that these statements will be said but not meant; that the repetition of them may conceal the necessity for grappling with the raw, indefinable, untidy experiences of real life. For it is there that the Word is to be met. The words of the creed are not the Word: they are words about the Word; and they may become so hollow for some who say them that they become words about nothing at all.

Consider, too, your systems of worship, designed to safeguard the moment and manner of the encounter with God. They are the means of worship, but not the end of worship. The baptism is a baptism of spirit; the feeding on Him is a feeding of the heart; the worship is an inward encounter beneath, beyond, without the symbols.

Consider, too, your structure of authority, designed to safeguard the community within which Christian love is to be learnt and through which Christian love is to be poured. Without some kind of authority, you say, there can be no liberty; and you are right: we have found it too. But authority is in the end deeper than the structure. Any man, meeting the unconditional, meets the challenge to obedience. It is God we obey, and sometimes your men in authority may speak God's word to us, sometimes they speak words that are not from God. But in any event, it is God we listen for, not man. No man, no human authority, is ever unconditional.

This is the kind of things Friends say, not as in the early days, with fluent pourings from the presses, but by the very fact that they live without creed and liturgy and priest, and still claim Christ. So long as the structured churches are open to the danger of overvaluing their structure, regarding it as end and not solely as means, so long there is need of this Quaker message to the churches, and for a group of Christians to live without the means. When the Church has learnt to hold them as means, the Society of Friends can wither away, its theme in the Christian symphony taken up by the whole orchestra.

So far the Quaker message emerges as a message to Christians, those discontented with their own forms and those not discontented enough. But to define the Quaker role in these terms alone would be to miss the most characteristic element, the most truly Christian element, in the whole story. What Friends have been doing, since the earliest days, in their quiet times as well as in their more vital times, has been to appeal 'to that of God in every man'. The Christian message, they would say, is not a message to Christians but a message to humanity. So long as Christians talk together—about their church order, about their worship and belief, about their domesticities—they are not telling the truth. It is only in their outward turning, as they penetrate the barriers human beings set up in their fear of each other and their fear of their own deepest lives, that the Christian Word is spoken. It is a Word 'beyond religion' to men and women 'beyond religion'. Christianity is mission.

But it is not, for Friends in their own vocation, 'missionary endeavour'. They have, from time to time and in many places, found themselves performing the conventional missionary task, with varying degrees of confidence or unease. But their hearts are not in preaching. Their idiom is rather service and reconciliation: meeting the needs of men and women stricken by war or natural disaster, bringing together men and women sundered by conflict and suspicion and ignorance. The characteristic activity is the 'Quaker centre' rather than the mission station. The 'centre' is simply a meeting point, in which the people round it, international diplomats, politicians, social workers, students, in such places as Geneva, Paris, and Delhi, can gather for talk and fellowship, in an atmosphere of trust: trust that they will not be proselytized, or 'got at' or over-persuaded, but just brought together to explore the human situation. 'Mission' here is not propaganda, at which Friends are unskilled and would remain unskilled, but conversation. It begins not in proclamation but in listening. It continues not in homiletic but in dialogue.

The dialogue is a serious dialogue, conducted in the spirit of Woolman's encounter with the Indians: 'that I might feel and understand their life, and the Spirit they live in, if haply I might receive some instruction from them, or they be in any degree helped forward by my following the Leadings of Truth amongst them'. The Quaker word to non-Christians is thus, to paraphrase George Fox,[1] 'The Buddha says this, the Prophet says this; what canst *thou* say?' The question of the 'truth' of other religions, with which many missionaries have been exercised, simply does not arise. All that matters is the insight gained by living men and women, the depth of their understanding of the human condition, the reality of their response to God. 'We believe,' says Gerald Hibbert,

> We believe in the divine initiative. We believe that, long before we began our missionary effort, God has visited the

[1] Margaret Fell quotes Fox as saying, 'You will say, Christ saith this, and the apostles say this; but what canst thou say?' 'The testimony of Margaret Fox concerning her late husband', in Fox's *Journal*, 1694, p. ii.

heart of every man and woman whom we may approach, preparing the way, calling, wooing, pleading. Our message of His actual presence already in every soul gives us wondrous hope and inspiration. This thought of the Divine Indwelling, so far from cutting the nerve of missionary effort in the case of early Friends, was the chief message which sent them forth. 'They gave their message with confidence, assured that God had visited the soul in advance to prepare the way for His truth. The word of God to Pascal: "Thou wouldst not seek Me, if thou hadst not already found Me", was in substance their philosophy of the conversion of any person' . . . It follows that we regard our missionary service as a working out *together* of a fuller and deeper conception of the nature and the life of God. It is a co-operative search and a co-operative finding—in a double sense. We co-operate with our fellows in seeking and finding God, and all the while we are co-operating with Him.[1]

Mission is not message, but meeting; not preaching but encounter, in which listening is as much an act of love as speaking. And if it be thought that such conversation offers an anaemic motive for world mission, the Friend would reply that to believe that God is infinite, and still to be sought, is better Christian theology than to believe he has been comprehended; and that to trust to the Holy Spirit is more orthodox than to speak about him.

This, in the end, would be the heart of the Quaker message to Christian and non-Christian alike: the challenge to trust in the Spirit of God. There is a proclamation and a theological proposition here: that the world is created and not a freak of chance; that man has a true being which it is his duty to find; that the witness to his being is already within him, ready to meet the voice of love; that no man is perfect in his love, that a Man once loved to perfection; that love is a living force, not to be described in formula or prescription, but still to be met, dangerous, unpredictable

[1] *The Christian Faith and Modern Missions,* 1933, pp. 27-8.

in its demands, but safe, worthy of trust in its truth and triumphant power.

The theology in all this remains, as it did in Fox's thought, implicit, inarticulate, naïve; and to the degree that it is naïve, Quakerism cannot stand alone, a church in its own right, carrying by itself the Christian meaning.

But if we try to answer the question, What is Christianity about? we shall have to answer that it is about not standing alone, about love in difference and not love in likeness—for do not the Gentiles the same? In the movement towards unity that springs from the insights so painfully acquired in the last three hundred years, there is need for all the strenuous thinking about belief and form and structure that the Church can produce; but there is need also for the naïve: the concentration on the moment, the raw experience, the felt simplicity. There is need for St Dominic, but there is also need for St Francis.

Friends make poor Dominicans, but they still sound the Franciscan note. They are unclear about what they 'believe in', but they are sure about what they 'trust to'. And the Christian faith is both a 'belief in' and a 'trust to'. This lay community of trusters may be carrying into the Church now moving toward unity an experience and a resolve which the structured denominations need for their new life.

Appendices

1 · THE SOCIETY OF FRIENDS TODAY

TABLE I

Statistics of Membership around the world[1]

AFRICA (40,808)

Burundi	1,172
East Africa	31,555
Madagascar	7,727
Other	354

ASIA (1,437)

India	395
Japan	276
Jordan and Lebanon	85
Taiwan	681

AUSTRALASIA (1,503)

Australia	893
New Zealand	610

EUROPE (24,334)

Denmark	53
France	135
Germany and Austria	539
Great Britain	21,289
Ireland	1,875
Netherlands	102
Norway	88
Sweden and Finland	142
Switzerland	111

NORTH AMERICA (124,054)

Canada	778
United States	123,276

SOUTH AND CENTRAL AMERICA (5,942)

Bolivia	3,000
Guatemala	1,479
Other	1,463

Total membership: 198,078

[1] From *Friends World News*, April 1964.

TABLE II

Adult Membership in Britain, 1963[1]

	Members			Elders and Overseers	
Quarterly Meeting	*Men*	*Women*	*Total*	*Men*	*Women*
Bedfordshire	566	736	1,302	93	127
Berks and Oxon	320	427	747	43	60
Bristol and Somerset	451	640	1,091	104	119
Cumberland	94	113	207	25	17
Derby, Lincoln and Notts	183	274	457	44	48
Devon and Cornwall	174	280	454	35	54
Durham	372	470	842	64	91
Essex and Suffolk	270	344	614	44	63
Kent	126	186	312	21	28
Lancs and Cheshire	730	898	1,628	128	161
London and Mddx	1,261	1,670	2,931	200	267
Norfolk, Cambs and Hunts	194	248	442	36	44
Scotland	158	214	372	25	35
Sussex, Surrey and Hants	680	1,073	1,753	109	191
Warwick, Leicester and Staffs	681	887	1,558	139	163
Western	421	499	920	74	91
Westmorland	137	190	327	19	42
Yorkshire	845	1,163	2,008	167	216
Totals	7,663	10,302	17,965[2]	1,372	1,817

2 · BOOKS FOR FURTHER READING

The history may be pursued, in outline, but with more detail than is given here, in my *The Discovery of Quakerism*, Harrap,

[1] From Reports and Documents presented to London Yearly Meeting, 1964.

[2] The discrepancy with Table I arises because the world figures show child members.

1960; and in still more detail in Elfreda Vipont's *The Story of Quakerism*, Bannisdale, 1960. The Rowntree Series of Quaker History, planned at the beginning of the century and published by Macmillan, are still the standard works:

Jones, Rufus M., *Studies in Mystical Religion*.
Jones, Rufus M., *Spiritual Reformers in the 16th and 17th Centuries*.
Braithwaite, William C., *The Beginnings of Quakerism*.
Jones, Rufus M., *The Quakers in the American Colonies*.
Braithwaite, William C., *The Second Period of Quakerism*.
Jones, Rufus M., *The Later Period of Quakerism*, 2 vols.

Discussions of Quaker thought are offered from time to time in the annual Swarthmore Lectures, published by George Allen and Unwin; and in A. Neave Brayshaw, *The Quakers, their story and message*, Allen and Unwin, 1953; Howard H. Brinton, *Friends for Three Hundred Years*, Allen and Unwin, 1953. More personal statements are Edgar B. Castle's *Approach to Quakerism*, Bannisdale, 1961, and my own *Friends Face Reality*, Bannisdale, 1954.

An anthology of Quaker writing, more vivid and readable than its title would suggest, is *Christian faith and practice in the experience of the Society of Friends*, London Yearly Meeting, 1960.

Journals and biographies are still the best ways of understanding Quakers. Fox's *Journal* is available in Everyman, and in a scholarly edition by John Nickalls, Cambridge, 1952. Woolman's *Journal* is also available in Everyman, which also publishes William Penn's *Some Fruits of Solitude*. An introductory anthology of short biographies is Stephen Allott's *Quaker Pioneers*, Bannisdale, 1963.

Books on Quakerism may be obtained from the Friends Book Centre, Euston Road, London, N.W.1; or Friends Book Store, 302 Arch Street, Philadelphia 6, Pa., USA. Questions would be dealt with, or forwarded to Friends who could deal with them, by George H. Gorman, Home Service Committee, Friends House, Euston Road, London, N.W.1; or Herbert M. Hadley, 152-A North 15th Street, Philadelphia 2, Pa., USA.

INDEX